Blessings

Ron Burgio

REVIVAL
Living in the SPIRIT of

A Pastor's Testimony
and Practical Applications for You

Ron Burgio quotes, 'The church should be an experience needing an explanation not an explanation needing an experience.' This book is one pastor's explanation of his church's incredible experience with revival. When you hear their story you can't help but want more of God for your life and church.

Mike Cavanaugh
Senior Pastor, Elim Gospel Church, Lima, NY

This is an easy-to-read account of one pastor's experience with revival. Having personally experienced the fire that broke out at Love Joy Gospel Church, and having known the integrity of my dear friend Ron Burgio for many years, it is with delight that I commend this fascinating story. What this church has touched will increase your hunger for God and enflame your heart for true biblical revival of historic proportions in this present hour.

Bob Sorge
Author, Teacher, Lee's Summit, MO

As my friend, Ron Burgio, shares about the challenges of being the pastor of a church during a time of revival, he talks about the dangers and the wonder of being the leader in a religious community that is experiencing a move of the Holy Spirit. He makes us know that this may well be the most difficult time of a leader's ministry in a local church. In this book, Pastor Burgio gives us not only his own life experience, but he also shares practical suggestions with any pastor who desires a genuine move of God in his ministry. This book is a "must" for any leader who desires to experience a move of God in their ministry. Mediocrity always challenges greatness, and radical Christianity always challenges the norm of ordinary church life. Let us prepare ourselves for the challenges that will face us when our people encounter God.

Tommy Reid,
Senior Pastor, The Tabernacle, Orchard Park, NY

Ron Burgio has captured in words the very essence of the work of the Holy Spirit as it happened in many parts of the world in the early 1990's. As one who was also impacted by the renewal in those days, I agree with the accounts presented in his book "Living in the Spirit of Revival." Pastor Burgio's testimony will serve for many years to come as a guide to other leaders who are pursuing the Lord and who find themselves in fresh visitations of the Holy Spirit. I have been stirred again to live in the spirit of revival and as you read the book for yourself, you too will be refreshed in the Spirit of the Lord.

Bernard J. Evans
President, Elim Fellowship, Lima, NY

Pastor Ron Burgio sought revival, found it, and did something every pastor needs to do. He sustained revival in his own life, his church, and in his ministry! God is using him powerfully around the world. Pastors need to hear and learn from his example if they truly desire to be used by God in the 21st Century Church!

John Shiver
Evangelist, Tampa, FL

In my reading of the account of Pastor Ron Burgio's trek through the years of renewal, I was blessed all over again. In my reading, I remembered many conversations we had during this time of blessing, when the events written in this book were taking place. Many of the chapters spoke of times and events in which I was personally involved. If anything, Ron Burgio actually understated many of the phases of visitation experienced by him and his church, not overstated. I recommend this book as an accurate account of the recent history of this vibrant, spirit-filled church. As the move of the Holy Spirit continues at Love Joy Gospel Church, the cry continues to be, "More Lord!"

Tom Brazell
Senior Pastor, Grace Chapel, Waycross, GA

For more than 30 years I have known Pastor Ron to be a man with an intense desire for all that God has. He has always been on the cutting edge, pursuing with fervency the move of God. This book reveals how a humble and dedicated servant of God can receive and distribute God's best. You will be blessed, encouraged, and inspired by this journey in revival.

Charles Pezzino
Senior Pastor, Creekside Gospel Temple, Amherst, NY

For those of you who have been waiting for a pastoral reflection on the current renewal, this is your book. Dr. Ron Burgio, a key influencer in our region and beyond, has pastored a church during wave upon wave of revival, and has put pen to paper to invite us into his journey. Ron's heart has been not just to change the people within his local church body, but to bring transformation to all the churches and structures of the region. If a temptation of renewal is to focus only on the success of 'my' church, then the author has resisted that temptation well. So I invite you to hear Ron's heart, catch his spirit, and invite the God who delights in giving good gifts to His children anew and afresh into your life, marriage, ministry, and city.

Al Warner
Set Free Buffalo, Buffalo, NY

In writing "Living in the Spirit of Revival," Dr. Ron Burgio is not presenting theory or wishful thinking. Ron's church has been touched by revival - lasting revival. The visitation of the Holy Spirit to Love Joy Gospel Church has been dynamic and no flash-in-the-pan event. During this ongoing visitation Ron has learned what it means to pastor a revival as he continues to pastor his church. The lessons he has learned and the resulting wisdom are invaluable for any church, church member or pastor wanting a visitation from God and wanting to know how to walk in that visitation when it comes.

David Mullen
Church of the Living God, Manchester, CT

REVIVAL
Living in the Spirit of

*A Pastor's Testimony
and Practical Applications for You*

DR. RON BURGIO

*Foreword by Paul Johansson
President, Elim Bible Institute*

K | KAIROS PUBLISHING

Living in the Spirit of Revival
Copyright © 2003 by Dr. Ron Burgio

Published by Kairos Publishing
PO Box 450
Clarence, NY 14031
www.kairos.us

Library of Congress Control Number: 2003103925

ISBN: 0-9665831-3-2

Cover & Interior Design: Peter Ecenroad

Editor: Dr. Larry Keefauver

Printed in the United States of America

TABLE OF CONTENTS

DEDICATION

To my beautiful wife,
Judy,
who through her faith, love, and dedication
is helping me to fulfill what God has ordained for me.

To ***Ray Sell***,
who ignited the fires of revival
in our lives at Love Joy Gospel Church.

ACKNOWLEDGMENTS

I am grateful to my secretary,
Uta Milewski,
for her research, editing, encouragement
and her attention to detail.

I also wish to express my appreciation to the people of
Love Joy Gospel Church
for trusting the Holy Spirit
as He led us into the unchartered waters of revival.
We will never be the same.

FOREWORD

R evival means different things to different people. In this book my friend, Ron Burgio, links revival to the outpouring of the Holy Spirit as in Acts 2, with signs following. Revival has been called renewal, even restoration. The songwriter of old said it well when he wrote, "Revive us again. Fill each heart with Thy love. May each soul be rekindled with the fire from above."

Revival can be the breathing of new life into that which is stagnant or fresh winds of the Spirit, or even cold water on the lips of the weary traveler. That which brings freshness and wholeness, and with it nourishes one's Spirit, has revival written all over it.

Before I proceed with my personal remarks on this book, let me relate to the reader my heartfelt appreciation for the author and his wife, Judy. Ron and Judy have been friends of my wife and me for the past 25 years. I have watched their growth as a family and maturing in the ministry. I am reminded of the words of Jesus to Nathaniel, "Behold an Israelite in whom there is no guile." What you see is what you get. Although Ron writes from his heart, it comes from spending time in prayer and the Word, searching for confirmations on each experience. I am deeply humbled by this opportunity to comment on his personal and spiritual pilgrimage.

For myself, having been exposed to the Latter Rain Movement in 1949 and the 50s, the Jesus people in the 60s, the Charismatic Movement in the 70s, and fresh waves since that time, I looked cautiously at the "renewal" of the 90s. When I saw the genuineness and balance in what God was doing with Pastor Ron and his church, Love Joy Gospel Church, in Buffalo, it helped me to sort out the "phony" from the genuine.

I am grateful for Ron's untiring effort to stay the Scriptural course in the midst of uncharted seas.

When the winds of revival sweep through a church, the "wind blows where it wants." I recognize that the wind is not given for direction, but for propelling. When these winds blow, there can be both reactions and responses to such outpouring. This is an account of one church and its experience with "strange or unusual" manifestations. The sum total is that the church is now more united, loving, hungry, and missions minded.

Revival is not the end result. It is the fresh impartation of the energy of the Spirit into a congregation so that it may move forward towards its God-given, unique destiny. This takes a very steady hand on the rudder of the ship so that even contrary winds can be used to bring the ship to its desired haven. Ron has shown himself a real helmsman.

Spiritual balance is not one event or another, but the total result of a conscious pursuit of Jesus as the Baptizer, who has fresh baptisms. We have been admonished by Paul to be "…filled with the Spirit." This is both personal and corporate. Indeed this book, in which Ron makes himself transparent, can give the reader a renewed passion for the freshness of the Holy Spirit. This book is not written as a manual for revival, but does provide some guidelines so that in the midst of the "mighty rushing wind" the ship moves forward into calm waters and is not driven into the rocks. Many who have missed this truth have found shipwreck, even though the wind was divine.

Take time to prayerfully meditate on this personal challenge to all of us - God has more, more than we could ask or think. May we never limit the Holy One of Israel.

Paul Johansson
President, Elim Bible Institute
Lima, NY

INTRODUCTION

During the thirty-one years I have been a Christian, I have frequently heard leaders consider the first century Church to be a model to which we should compare our contemporary church life.

In my early years of pastoring, I rarely witnessed the signs and wonders that were a reality in the early Church. I had heard how God moved in revivals of the past, and I read about signs and wonders in the Book of Acts, but I wanted to experience revival myself. I wanted to see miracles, to experience His presence, and be spiritually empowered to minister more effectively. I was desperate for God to show up in my life and in our local church.

This book is a testimony to show that God is not a respecter of persons or churches, and when He is sincerely invited, He will come and have His way.

The Body of Christ has different ways of expressing itself. One church may emphasize *holiness and intimacy with God*, *another the sovereign outpouring of God's Spirit upon His hungry people*, and yet another *evangelism and winning people to Christ*. I believe we need to flow in unity with them all. If God has specifically called us to one stream, then by His grace and power, we need to do all we can to be that type of church; but why not have it all?

I believe that God has called me to pastor a church with signs, wonders, miracles, presence, and power. Simultaneously, He wants to empower our church to affect families, neighborhoods, cities, countries and the world. I have found that God's visitation in our church is not only for evangelism and for bringing change and holiness to people, but it is also for the demonstration of His glory in the Church.

CHAPTER 1

A HEART FOR REVIVAL

"Fill her, Lord!" Ray Sell shouted as he approached Kate, a woman from our congregation. She was standing near the back in the packed sanctuary of our church. Ray had barely even touched her when she slumped down to the ground in the center aisle. She began to laugh hysterically. I was stunned and so were the people around us. I knew Kate, and she, of all people, was one who had it together. She was intelligent, educated, well traveled and self-controlled. She and her husband had been missionaries for years. What was happening with her?

Ray, dressed in a black suit with a bold, colorful tie, had just preached at our church for the first time. I had met him the day before and liked him immediately. He was young, stylish, enthusiastic and as energetic as any evangelist I'd known. He had left his pastorate in Florida to bring revival to the churches in the North East. I hoped church would not be business as usual that Sunday, but I was surprised that this was really happening.

I had watched Rodney Howard-Browne on TV, and expected something similar from Ray's ministry. So, being the pastor and seeing my own church members rolling on the floor, laughing, I knew we were in for a ride. However, I sensed God's presence like never before. I went along with Ray as he prayed for more people.

Leading a church through the excitement and turbulence of renewal is an adventure. In this book, I want to take you through my adventure, so that you can be inspired and in some ways equipped when God does a new thing in your church. Eleven years earlier, the Lord had started to prepare me.

Prepare for Revival

In 1983, while co-pastoring a local church in Williamsville, New York, I heard of Bob Bosworth, a man of God who had a ministry of early morning prayer. At that time, he was holding a training week of prayer at a church pastored by a friend of mine on Grand Island.

Pray. I always had a desire to pray for at least an hour each day, but seldom was I able to pray consistently. I cried out to God, "Lord, I want to be involved in what You are involved in."

God spoke to my heart, "Ron, I want you to be involved in what I'm doing, but I want you to be prepared in your heart so I can use you in that day."

As I attended the training, it became a transforming experience. I received revelation on the importance of early morning prayer and the grace (the desire and ability) to actually do it. As I began to pray, I was enabled to enter His presence, and it was there that I was saturated with His love. For the first time in my life, prayer became exciting. Little did I know that early morning prayer was going to prepare me for what God would have in store, just one year later.

Wait on God. I learned to wait on the Lord, and as I began to do so, a renewing and an empowering began to occur in my life. The Lord not only says, "Come to Me," He also says, "Abide in Me."

During that powerful hour each day, I waited on the Lord and interceded for those He put on my heart. It was a time of being alone with Him; a time that from then on, I seldom missed. Even traveling overseas or on family vacations, I always remained disciplined in early morning prayer.

Our church services in Williamsville were held on Saturday nights, which left Sunday mornings open for me to seek the Lord. Each Sunday morning, my focus of prayer would be for the churches of local pastor friends who met in Buffalo and Western New York.

In the spring of 1984, my wife, Judy and I, both had a sense that God was preparing us for a change in ministry. We believed that He was preparing us to pastor our own church. We began to pray and fast, and we implored God to move us by His Spirit. We told Him that we were available, but that we did not want to go anywhere unless He called us out supernaturally.

Tom Brazell, founding Pastor of Love Joy Gospel Church, was on a short-term missions trip to Zaire (now the Congo).

While there, the Lord called him to leave the pastorate and minister in Zaire. After some inner struggle, he told the Lord that he would be glad to minister in Zaire as long as the Lord would both, provide a shepherd for Love Joy, and also speak to his wife about moving to Africa. The Lord immediately gave him my name as the next pastor. The Lord also spoke to his wife, Judy Brazell. Not only was she prepared to go to Africa by the time Tom came back home, but she also knew that I would be the next pastor. A few days after Tom's return, we met for lunch, and he offered me the pastorate at Love Joy Gospel Church. I was speechless.

Judy and I took some time to pray and fast about our decision. At the end of our three-day fast we received our own word from the Lord. He gave us not only an inner witness, but also the following Scripture: *"For you shall go out with joy, and be led out with peace; the mountains and the hills shall break forth into singing before you, and all the trees of the field shall clap their hands. Instead of the thorn shall come up the cypress tree, and instead of the brier shall come up the myrtle tree; and it shall be to the LORD for a name, for an everlasting sign that shall not be cut off"* (Isaiah 55:12-13).

Paul Brenton, the pastor I worked with at Williamsville Christian Fellowship, was gracious to release about twenty adults and ten children to help us build Love Joy Gospel Church, which had twenty-five members at that time. These people and the solid apostolic foundation Tom Brazell had laid, enabled Judy and me to have faith that we would be successful in our new ministry. The combined leadership and resources were in place for the Holy Spirit to use for God's glory.

On the morning of Sunday, July 29, 1984, the first day I was to preach as pastor of Love Joy Gospel Church, God challenged me to continue to pray each Sunday for the pastors in the city. He asked me, "Do you now feel that they are your competition, or will you continue to support and pray for them?" I made the choice to continue praying for them and not to consider any pastor or church ever to be my competition.

Envision. God then gave me a clear vision of His mandate for Love Joy Gospel Church. In a vision, I first saw a map of the Buffalo area, then I saw streets and houses, and then people. God spoke within my spirit that we could win Buffalo for Christ. I knew that this vision was not just an opportunity for me to cooperate with God, but that God, myself, and other pastors would work together to win Buffalo for Christ.

A number of people from my new congregation met with me weekly for an early morning prayer meeting to seek God, and ask Him to fulfill His plans through us.

Hear God's Voice. While I was reading Psalm 31:8, God told me that He would set my feet in a large place. This word was confirmed many times through different people. In September of 1985, Rev. Harold Harding spoke the following prophecy over Love Joy Gospel Church:

> *I have not called thee to look upon thy possibilities and say, 'What shall we do?' but I have called thee to know that I am the Lord that reigneth. I have called thee to look upon the needs, and plan and prepare according to the needs, not according to thine ability. For I will yet*

*be a provider unto thee, and I will yet require of thee
things that your mind has not yet thought of, and I
would ask of thee to prepare for yet an ingathering. And
where your mind has said that you have been few for so
long, yet I say, 'Am I the Lord of few, or am I the Lord
of many?'*

*Therefore, know that that which mine hand purposes for
thee, so am I able to do. Therefore, change thy vision
and change thy thinking from the few unto the many,
and begin to enlarge the vision within thine heart, within thy spirit. For yea, I have come unto thee, and I will
do a work in thee, and I will expand thy borders, and I
will cause thy tent straps to be lengthened, and thou
shall be estranged from thy present situation, and ye
shall find yourself in a large place.*[1]

Pray Together and Abide. I continued to pray early each
morning. My personal prayer times were rich with the presence
of the Lord. I learned to encourage myself in the Lord and to
overcome every obstacle, but I wanted my congregation to also
abide and pray the same. I longed for them to become strong in
prayer. I preached about prayer. I taught about prayer. I told the
people that the reason many Christians are not experiencing the
power that the New Testament talks about is because they are
lacking in their prayer life.

Many were frustrated because of a lack of fruitfulness in their
lives and ministry. I taught them that praying only out of duty,
with a disregard to relationship and fellowship with the Lord, was

ineffective. I knew that the true purpose of prayer was to lead us to the person of Jesus, the Living Word.

Andy Zack, who is now my associate pastor, was at this time pastoring Full Gospel Community Church in Warsaw, New York. Andy told me about a set of teaching tapes by Dr. Larry Lea, *Could You Not Tarry One Hour?* Larry Lea's materials were designed to transform prayer from desire, to discipline, to delight. As he says, "God is calling His Church to pray, but for too many of God's people, prayer is a lost art. The desire to pray is not something we can work up in our flesh. The desire must be birthed in us by the Holy Spirit, a divine desire implanted by the Spirit of God in our hearts."[2]

Dr. Lea uses the Lord's Prayer as a model with six topics on which to expand during daily prayer. He writes, "In this model prayer now known as 'The Lord's Prayer,' Jesus also enumerated topics and instructed: 'After this manner therefore pray ye' (Matthew 6:9-13). We have memorized, quoted, and sung the Lord's Prayer, but we have not seen it as a group of six topics to be followed in prayer under the guidance of the Holy Spirit."[3]

I found in this material the "handle" needed for teaching our people to pray daily, to pray for an extended period of time, and to pray effectively.

Growth. We saw our church grow from twenty-five to one hundred within three years. In 1987 we outgrew our facility and purchased a banquet hall on Walden Avenue in Cheektowaga, New York. I knew that God wanted my feet to be in a large place, and when we prepared the sanctuary on Walden Avenue, I was amazed at how large it was. God, however, was not that impressed. He told me clearly, "This is not the large place."

I moved my family into a house right behind the church. Each Sunday morning I walked to the church at six o'clock and prayed for God's presence to saturate the building. I longed for His presence. I prayed for it each week and we could sense Him in our services. New people were added to our church every month, and I soon became concerned that numerical growth was outpacing spiritual growth.

Build Strong Foundations

The Lord spoke to me and said that there was a lack in the foundations. I knew what He meant. In order to have a stronger church, everything needs to be built on a strong foundation, just like in the construction of a home.

Teach Sound Doctrine. We needed to build the spiritual foundation of our people. When I mentioned this to Rev. Paul Stern, a personal friend and encourager, he introduced me to *The Foundations Course*. I felt the Lord tell me that we needed to make a midcourse correction and begin grounding our people in the basic fundamental doctrines and teachings of the Scriptures.

Equip Leaders. We started in 1989, by putting the leadership of the church through *The Foundations Course*. Since then, everyone who wants to serve at Love Joy is required to complete this twelve-week course. We have gained valuable stability through this process. It has become a great way to see if the people are committed to serve in our church and be faithful in their attendance. Once they have completed the course, we know that they would have learned the foundational principles of the faith, truths about our local church governmental structure, the role of the pastors as equippers, and the role of the congregational members as ministers. *The Foundations Course* promoted unity in our church and helped the pastoral staff get to know each new member in a more personal way.

PREPARING FOR REVIVAL REQUIRES TIME, COMMITMENT AND DIRECTION

As you begin to live in revival, remember these keys:

Prepare yourself, as you:

- Pray
- Wait on God
- Envision
- Hear God's Voice
- Pray Together and Abide
- Get Ready to Grow Numerically and Spiritually
- Build Strong Foundations
- Teach Sound Doctrine
- Equip Leaders

CHAPTER 2

STEPS TO REVIVAL

As we moved toward revival, some visible signs began to appear. Attendance continued to increase, and though we had already expanded the sanctuary once, we still had no parking lot of our own. Sunday school classroom space was very tight and some of the classrooms were located right above the sanctuary. Sunday after Sunday, my sermons were accompanied by the pitter-patter of little feet, which at times sounded like a thunderstorm.

We considered purchasing an existing building, but after searching unsuccessfully, we decided to build. In order to build a church we needed to raise money. God led us to a consultant, Fred Whittey, to conduct a stewardship campaign. The *United in Purpose* campaign was a great success in several respects.

Vision for growth and expansion filled us with excitement and anticipation. We began to believe for "the invisible" that was not yet seen but which God pictured for us in our hearts. People soon became excited about a piece of land and a church building that we did not yet have but believed God to provide. The campaign enabled us not only to maintain the unity of the church, but heightened it as we worked together for God's purpose.

Revival requires sacrifice. The campaign caused "the cream to rise to the top" in our congregation. A number of members discovered the calling and gifting that God had given them, and some of these people are now key leaders in our church. The campaign ran for three years, and from 1992 to 1995, a total of 116 families sacrificed $292,000 towards our new building. Our consultant, Fred Whittey, said that revival will not come unless we sacrifice. Our people were willing to sacrifice.

Revival requires faith. In April of 1993 about eighty percent of the congregation committed themselves to listen to the New Testament on tape every day for one month during the *Faith Comes By Hearing* campaign. This dramatically increased their time in God's Word. I preached on faith, and we felt God raise our faith level and our expectations.

God continued to cause growth numerically, yet I felt as though I was starving spiritually. We had a large church numbering from two hundred to two hundred-fifty. The praise and worship was inspiring, the leadership was excellent, and the congregation was excited, but I felt like there was a famine for God's presence and for His miracles. I wanted to see what had happened in the Book of Acts and what had gone on in past revivals. For years I had been crying out to God for revival; for years I wondered what it would be like if the heavens opened and God visited us with His glory.

Revival requires hunger. The Lord continued to increase my desire and caused me to cry out for revival as never before. I began to preach and prophesy, "There is the sound of the abundance of rain" (I Kings 18:41). The Bible says, "Blessed are the people who know the joyful sound." I began to hear it in the Spirit, but I also wanted to know and experience it. My ministry credentials are through Elim Fellowship in Lima, New York, where I also serve as an elder, and more recently, as Vice President.

In early February of 1994, at a Council of Elders meeting at the Fellowship Headquarters in Lima, my friend and fellow elder, Gerald Tricket, shared about a wonderful experience he had recently encountered. He began by telling us that after twenty-seven years in ministry, he had been so discouraged, that he had wanted to quit. During a vacation in Florida some friends took him to a Rodney Howard-Browne meeting in Lakeland. At first he was skeptical, but then he began to sense the presence of the Lord. He saw the people around him getting touched and asked, "Lord, what about me? Can I get touched?" In turn, the Holy Spirit asked him, "Are you ready?"

During the next meeting, Rodney Howard-Browne said, "There is a minister here who is really discouraged. He is even considering giving up the ministry. I would like you to come forward." Gerald jumped up and ran to the front. He got to within twenty feet of the platform and felt the power of God hit him like a two-by-four plank of lumber. He literally fell to the floor right in the middle of the aisle. He shared with us that the touch of God renewed, revived, and set him free from all the despondency he had been feeling.

Revival requires an anticipation of signs and wonders. Gerald told us about signs and wonders, laughter, salvations, healings and miracles. He laid hands on us and prayed for us. He also told us about a young evangelist that had come to his church. His name was Ray Sell. Ray was affiliated with Rodney's Ministry and had brought that same refreshing to Gerald's church. I was impressed and excited.

I now felt that this was what I had been waiting for, and I was hungrier than ever. I knew I wanted to have this young man come to our church to ignite the kindling that had been prepared in our hearts.

Revival requires desperation. A few days after this meeting, when Andy Zack and I prayed for my secretary, Uta Milewski, she reacted as if drunk, to the point where she could hardly remain standing or continue working. We had never seen anyone "drunk in the Spirit" and were all very surprised.

I invited Ray to come to Buffalo. He was scheduled to be with us in April of 1994. From the time I extended the invitation, I was nervous, because, as I began to watch Rodney Howard-Browne on television, I wasn't so sure how all the laughter and falling out was going to go over at my church. Nevertheless, my desperation for God was greater than my concern that the people might not like it.

Revival requires preparation. In the spring of 1994, we did a *Fifty-Day Adventure* together. This is a program of fifty daily devotions for adults, youth and children followed up with pulpit preaching on specific themes. From February 13 until March 27,

I preached sermons relating to the weekly readings. Little did I know that God was causing us to prepare the way for a wonderful move of His Spirit just a few weeks later.

One week before Ray Sell was to come to our church, I felt the need to preach a message to help our people receive what God would bring to us. I studied the second chapter of Acts and prepared a sermon called *Preparation for Revival*. Before I preached it on April 3, 1994, during the praise and worship, one of our longtime members, Jimmy Rey, had a message in tongues. The following interpretation came through Mike Marinelli:

> *"The Lord would say to His people, 'Just like a young man waits for his bride to walk down the long aisle, yea, know, the Lord longs to be with his bride. He is extremely excited and when the Father says, 'Go!' will He not come quickly? Do you not see that He is jumping up and coming to the bride to bring her to Himself, to have fellowship, to be joyful, to be happy, to be at peace?' Yea, the Lord would say, 'Are you ecstatic, are you anticipating, are you waiting for Me? Truly a union will come between My bride and Me, and it will be a great union. The whole heavens will be ecstatic and happy. Yea, I will come quickly. This union will be great. Yea, even as the universe has never seen, the union will be great.'"* [4]

Different People React Differently to Revival

In my sermon, I talked about the three different reactions of those who witnessed the outpouring of the Holy Spirit at Pentecost. I used as my text Acts 2:1-21. Those present were waiting for something to happen, but they were not all ready for what really would take place.

The Skeptics. Some who came that day were skeptics. They mocked (v.13).

The Spectators. Some were spectators who just came to see what was happening (v. 12).

The Spirit-filled. Then, there were those who received freely from the Lord and were filled with the Spirit and the power of God (v. 4). They went out and changed the course of history. They changed their families, their surroundings, and the world.

I also gave these words of encouragement:
> This move of God is real.
> Expect the unexpected.
> Be ready to receive from the Lord, personally.
> Be more aware of what God is doing in *you* than what He is doing in others.
> Be prepared for your flesh to rise up.
> The carnal is always set against the Spirit.
> God is going to do a work in our lives that will help us in the days ahead.
> God is looking for a people who are on fire and are able to carry the message.

Don't judge what you are not used to, but respond to the Scriptures and what the Holy Spirit is saying.

Seek the Lord before the meetings to move not only in your own life but also in all who come.

Pray for the presence of the Lord to be here in an awesome way.

The *Preparation for Revival* sermon classic preached by C.H. Spurgeon at the Metropolitan Tabernacle in London on October 30, 1864, became an inspiration for me personally. I would go back to it again and again during renewal meetings and highlight one point or another.

There were always new people who needed to hear it. Some of them were newly saved; others were visitors from other churches. Whenever I preach a series of revival meetings at other churches, I like to start with this sermon.

When I preached this sermon the first time that April morning, I was stepping out in faith, expecting God to do great things in the coming week. Our congregation received the message, and I believe it helped them to receive from God when He began to move by His Spirit.

Revival is a Sovereign Move of God

I look back now and see how God led us from early morning prayer in 1984, to praying for the other churches and pastors in Western New York, through the *United in Purpose* campaign, daily listening to the Word on tape, through the *Fifty-Day*

Adventure, and to the prophetic words He gave us so that we would be prepared to receive what He was about to do.

In *Preparation for Revival*, Spurgeon observed:

> *Now, dear friends, we need as the first and most essen-*
> *tial thing in this matter, that God should walk with us.*
> *In vain we shall struggle after revival unless we have*
> *His presence.*
>
> *If, then, we desire to have His presence with us, we*
> *must see to it that we are perfectly agreed with Him*
> *both in the design of the work, and in the method of it;*
> *and I desire this morning to stir up your pure minds to*
> *heart-searching and vigilant self-examination, that*
> *every false way may be purged from us, since God will*
> *not walk with us as a Church, unless we be agreed with*
> *Him.*

I am both amazed and overwhelmed by the sovereign leading of God's Spirit in our church's life. We were just a small church in an unpretentious area of town, but God saw a people who would obey Him, and who would allow His Presence to move on them in a marvelous way.

We discovered as God had promised that blessing and prosperity touches His people when they love and obey Him. "So if you faithfully obey the commands I am giving you today, to love the LORD your God and to serve him with all your heart and with all your soul, then I will send rain on your land in its season, both autumn and spring rains, so that you may gather in your grain, new wine and oil. I will provide grass in the fields for your cattle, and you will eat and be satisfied" (Deut. 11:13-15 NIV).

WHAT DOES REVIVAL REQUIRE?

As you take God-directed steps toward revival individually and corporately in your church, remember that:

Revival Requires:

- Sacrifice
- Faith
- Hunger
- Anticipation of Signs and Wonders
- Desperation
- Preparation
- A Willingness for God to move Sovereignly in your Life and in your Church

Chapter 3

Revival Comes

O n Sunday, April 10, 1994, as I stepped onto the platform before approximately two hundred people, I could feel the anticipation in the church.

Ray Sell preached an excellent message about being hungry for God. After the message, he invited the Holy Spirit to come. And He came! Soon the place was filled with the manifest presence of God and people began to fall to the floor without Ray even coming near them.

Ray then walked off the platform and began to pray for many people and laid hands on them. I went along with him and caught them as they fell to the floor. It was quite an amazing morning. Twenty to thirty people got saved or rededicated their lives.

That Sunday night we had our first evening meeting, and again God's presence was powerfully manifested. I started to catch for Ray after the preaching because I wasn't really sure what else to do.

As I went with him, I saw people genuinely going down under the power of the Holy Spirit. Many fell without him even touching them, and if he did touch them, it was just a slight laying on of his hand on their head or chest. After I had caught about fifteen people, Ray turned to me and said, "Be filled." I immediately went down under the power and fell to the floor. As I lay there, the presence and the joy of the Lord came, and I found myself laughing and being set free in my spirit. It literally really felt as though rivers of living water were flowing out of my innermost being.

God was bathing me in His love; I was lost in His presence, filled with joy, and drunk in the Holy Spirit. From that point on I was hooked and I couldn't get enough.

Manifestations of God's Presence

My secretary, Uta Milewski, shared her experiences with me in writing, "I found Ray's preaching funny, engaging, and laced with down-to-earth humor. I had never heard someone say that I needed to be hungry for God. I was used to hearing that I needed to be content. When Ray finished preaching, he stepped off the platform and prayed, 'Holy Spirit of God, you have told me, that if I made room for you to move, you would come and manifest yourself. I will not stop you; I will not hinder you. Holy Spirit of God, come NOW!'"

"Across the aisle from me, Helen, Pastor Ron's mother-in-law, crashed to the floor. In front, a woman's uplifted hand started to flutter wildly. 'What is this?' I wondered. Tom Giambra, who stood two pews ahead of us, swayed dangerously. Ray gently pulled the woman out of the pew. He placed his hand on her forehead and shouted, 'Fill, fill, fill... More, more...'

Physical Manifestations of His Presence. "I could see her starting to lean back a little. Ray called out, 'I need an usher here!' The woman was already falling backwards when the usher stepped up and caught her. Her hands continued to flutter and shake. I had seen people being slain in the Spirit before.

"My first Christian meeting had been a charismatic conference with Benny Hinn in 1979. This was different, though. This woman fell and didn't jump right back up. She just stayed on the floor, shaking and fluttering.

"Tom was next. Ray touched his forehead, shouted 'Fill!' and Tom crashed down. I was a little annoyed with the way Ray shouted. It was a little uncomfortable to see people lose control and crash to the floor. Tom started to weep. I could hear him where I was. Kate Nash keeled over when Ray touched her. She immediately started to break out in the most liberating, hilarious laughter. Kate is not usually one to be out of control, but right then and there she lost all dignity and decorum. She writhed on the floor in laughter.

"Ray continued from person to person, never saying anything but 'Fill' or 'More.' That evening, after Ray preached, I watched again as he was laying hands on people. By now I was fascinated with the different manifestations. It was funny seeing people laugh and lose their stiff reserve. I wanted to experience it for myself. When Ray prayed for me, I could sense my legs becoming wobbly, my body become heavy, and somehow I lost the connection to my legs. I didn't know anymore how to stand up, and it didn't matter. I fell to the floor and stayed there for a while. Suddenly Ray's shouting didn't bother me anymore. Instead with each 'Fill' and 'More' I felt God's presence invade me more."

The Manifest Desire to Make God Known to Others

All of us experienced what my secretary sensed. Encountering God at this level created within me the desire to make Him known to others in the same way. All I desired was for people to know God-the One whose presence brings fullness of joy. I spent every free moment during that first revival week calling my pastor friends in the Western New York area and telling them to come and check it out for themselves.

Ray told me to invite them for Friday morning when we would have a special emphasis on five-fold ministry leaders. Ray told me that the laying on of hands would transfer this same anointing to others. I was the first in line to get prayer that Friday morning. Ray had talked about a *Mack Truck* experience with the Holy Spirit. He had explained that when a *Mack Truck* hits you, you're never the same again. Well, I was hit that morning. After Ray prayed for me and I was lying on the floor, God spoke to me.

He asked, "Ron, what would you like Me to do for you?" The first thing I thought of was that I needed healing in my feet. I had experienced painful heel spurs for a while, and the only thing that could be done in the natural was to operate. So I asked the Lord, "Would you heal my feet?" I was on the floor for over three hours, and when I got up, my feet were free of pain and are totally healed to this day.

The Manifestation of Joy

Friday night we announced that we had extended the meetings for another week, and the people responded with great joy. That evening, Ray encouraged me to start praying for my people. At first I wondered if anything would happen at all. My doubts were quickly eased when person after person was filled with joy. Pretty soon we had to stack up all of the chairs in the sanctuary because we ran out of floor space. Later, while Andy Zack played the guitar and sang, spontaneous dancing broke out, even while some people still lay sprawled out on the floor. It turned into a holy party filled with exuberant joy.

During these two weeks, we saw our church filled to over three hundred people every night and over a hundred each morning. We witnessed miraculous healings and wild deliverances, and we rejoiced as scores came to the altar to give or rededicate their hearts to Christ.

As word spread, people came from all over the city and suburbs to witness what God was doing. Our worship became even more free and intimate. Many received from the Lord and brought it back to their own churches.

Right from the start Ray encouraged people to bring their friends. He especially asked us to bring those with incurable diseases. Peter and Kate Nash knew of a family with a young girl who had cancer. Her prognosis was so hopeless that her parents had already bought a grave site. She had a football-sized tumor in her abdomen and the doctors were planning on doing one last surgery to slow her cancer down.

The Manifestation of Healing

The girl's surgery was scheduled for late April. They came to the revival service on Tuesday night. The whole family was there: mom, dad and seven children. Ray laid hands on the girl and soaked her in prayer for quite a while. The rest of the family also received prayer. From then on her dad brought her to every meeting. Often Ray would pray for her even before he began preaching, and she would just lie there for hours, soaking in the tangible presence of the Lord. Ray said, "She's receiving Holy Ghost chemotherapy." The night before the scheduled surgery at Roswell Park Cancer Institute, her little sister had a vision that when the doctors would open her up, they would be amazed.

The report came the day after surgery: The tumor was gone, and she was cancer free. This was fully documented at the hospital. We had quite a celebration during our next Sunday service.

The Manifest Desire to Be In His Presence

I felt we needed to have an ongoing service each week set aside specifically for renewal. I was more confident now that God would flow through me and the other pastors on staff.

We started first with a Sunday night service and later switched to Wednesday nights. We had planned to keep Sunday mornings "business as usual," but from that time on, Sunday morning services were far from ordinary.

We were like people living in a new world where the presence of God was so tangible it was as if we could see Him face to face.

People were being saved every week. For about two years we had continual, four week *New Believers'* classes taught by Janet Wereski.

The Manifestation of Deliverance

We found that some people who had struggled with issues and had been in counseling began to be set free quicker after attending renewal meetings. I had always believed in deliverance, and I had, since early in my ministry ministered deliverance to people.

Now I began to have greater confidence that our elders and others on our ministry team could minister deliverance as well.

Revival Renews

People throughout our whole church were being renewed. I was personally renewed. Since then the presence of God has been flowing in an awesome way in all of our lives. My elders were touched, the worship team and my staff were all renewed, and most of our lay leaders were touched. Some people were skeptical, some were cautious, a few mocked, but most wanted to receive.

Leadership Renewal. I had kept the Council of Elders at Elim Fellowship in Lima, New York informed about our meetings. I was also able to arrange for Ray Sell to preach at Elim Bible Institute and Elim Gospel Church where he ministered for about three weeks. In her book, *Elim - Living in the Flow* , Edith Adele Veach recorded the impact of Ray Sell's ministry:

"But there was a fresh current moving, and like Elim's founder, [Ivan Q. Spencer], L. Dayton Reynolds [General Overseer from 1989-1997] wanted to be a part of it, and he received his first opportunity in 1994. During a council of elders meeting at Elim Fellowship, Elder Gerald Trickett of Sterling Heights, Michigan, shared about his experience at Carpenter's Home Church and at his own church, Joy Community. Gerald witnessed firsthand the revival in Lakeland, Florida, attending services there in January of 1994. He met a brother there, Ray Sell, who had been greatly impacted by Rodney Howard-Browne's ministry. Being originally from Michigan, Ray told Gerald that he felt God was going to bring the revival there. Consequently, Gerald invited Ray to minister, resulting in meetings a month later where God sovereignly moved upon the congregation just as He had been moving in Argentina, Florida, and Toronto. As Gerald began to tell the elders of Elim what had transpired at his own church, Dayton asked, 'Brother, please pray for me. I don't want to miss what God is doing in this hour.'"

"With that Brother Trickett prayed for not just Dayton but for the whole council of elders. Ron Burgio, one of the elders at the meeting, requested Ray's phone number, and later arranged for Brother Sell to minister at his church, Love Joy Gospel Church, in Buffalo, New York. Miraculous things happened when Sell went there. Meeting twice a day, six days a week for two weeks, God moved upon the people. They saw a young girl suffering from cancer radically healed; doctors even documented it. Burgio called Mike Cavanaugh and reported what had been happening, and so Mike invited Ray to come to Elim Gospel Church."

"During the meetings Brother Sell held at Elim Gospel Church, the Annual Ministers' Conference for Elim Fellowship was happening. Ray was asked to minister at one of the sessions for the conference. God gloriously moved. Leadership for the fellowship along with other credential holders were strewn across the tabernacle's floor "under the power of the Holy Ghost." Sounds of laughter, praise, and tongues broke out as God moved among the Elim constituency. From there, Brother Sell's ministry impacted other Elim churches in New York, Massachusetts, and Canada. Elim once again, was in the flow of God's visitation, and Dayton Reynolds had the awesome opportunity of being there."[5]

Personal Renewal. He then came back to Buffalo and ministered at some churches here and then went to Southern Ontario, Canada. I went to as many of his meetings as I could. I continued to get touched and filled and changed. It was not just falling down and laughing. Real change happened in areas of my life where I had been struggling.

I found the Lord setting me free and releasing me that I might serve Him. The Word of God became more real to me. Hunger for the Word and prayer intensified in my life. When I read the Word, the Holy Spirit revealed things to me in new and marvelous ways.

Church Renewal. Ray said that church should be an experience needing an explanation, not an explanation needing an experience. I began to search the Word for the explanation for what was happening to us. The Holy Spirit opened the Scriptures to me and led me to many passages that I had never fully understood.

Before this, I had never even heard about what was happening in Toronto. It wasn't until May or June of 1994, that I found out about the "Toronto Blessing." All I can say is, that we were having a "Buffalo Blessing" at Love Joy Gospel Church. Since then, of course, we have heard that God was moving all over the world. I'm just grateful that as we opened the door, the Holy Spirit came in. As a result, many doors opened up for me to do revival meetings in our region, in different parts of the country, and in other nations. There was a fresh anointing on me as I went out to preach, and the gifts of healing and prophecy were flowing freely.

When I preached at churches in the Buffalo area, I would often bring our worship team and members of our staff to help me minister. During ministry time, God moved and we would pray and soak the people in the presence of God.

WHEN RENEWAL COMES...

Revival Renewal Manifests:

- God's Presence Physically
- As a Desire to make God known To Others
- Joy, Healing and Deliverance

Revival Renews:

- Pastors and Leaders Personally
- Whole Congregations
- Congregation to Congregation

CHAPTER 4

REVIVAL SURVIVAL

O ne night, during our first week of revival, after lying on the floor and resting in God's presence, I sat up and looked across the sanctuary to where Judy, my wife, was standing. She glared at me. Still drunk in the Spirit, I didn't understand what was going on, but something was definitely wrong.

After we talked, I began to understand. The presence of God had stirred up some things she had been holding in for a long time. She confronted me about our relationship: about the time I spent away from home, and my lack of communication with her. Suddenly, I realized that my relationship with Judy wasn't as good as I thought it was. I repented, and agreed to go through counseling with her.

We learned to communicate better, speak the truth in love to one another, repent, forgive and move on. Thank God that in the passion and excitement of what was happening in the church, I didn't ignore what Judy said. I realized that God was bringing up these weaknesses in order to deal with them. For a while it looked like revival would wreck our marriage, but we were committed to work on our relationship until it once again became a source of joy. We are God's unbeatable, inseparable, husband and wife team.

I enjoyed bringing this fresh move of God to churches that had not yet experienced it. Sometimes the pastors were all for it, but the people were unsure how to receive it. A pastor in Southern Ontario had scheduled me to come and preach for a week. One day before the meetings, he told me that his people were the "frozen chosen," and he hoped that God would move in and melt the resistance. I felt challenged and excited as I preached my *Preparation For Revival* sermon and brought the people into the presence of God. I taught them to expect God to meet them and fill them with the Holy Spirit. My time there was very fruitful.

At another church the people were ready to receive, but the leadership was reluctant. I worked very hard, but found it difficult to minister freely.

Revival flows when leaders are receptive. From these two experiences, I learned that receptivity of the pastors and elders in the church is key to the anointing, and in understanding the meaning of Psalm 133. "Behold, how good and how pleasant it is for brethren to dwell together in unity! It is like the precious oil upon the head, running down on the beard, the beard of Aaron, running down on the edge of his garments. It is like the dew of Hermon, descending upon the mountains of Zion; for there the LORD commanded the blessing life forevermore."

The pastors and elders of the church have to open the gates in order for God to move. I am so grateful that our pastors and elders did that for Love Joy Gospel Church.

Having learned this important lesson, I put my energies into keeping the unity of faith within our staff, our eldership, and our own church. I taught and preached on unity. I spoke with church members who were spreading divisive comments, persuading them to voice any complaints or questions to me instead of to the congregation. Some people just had honest questions about what God was doing, but others questioned what I was doing.

Revival makes some uncomfortable. When I encouraged people to receive prayer and yield to God, some didn't like it. They were uncomfortable with the manifestations of falling and laughing and came to me and asked me to stop it all. After a couple of months, they wanted to go back to the way things had been. I could not go back, but as their shepherd I needed to know the condition of my flock, and I encouraged my leaders to be honest with me about what they felt and thought.

God Uses Particular People to Welcome Revival

It's important for me to reflect on this particular moment in time when God broke into our lives and gave us revival. We experienced divine visitation that had both powerfully positive effects and a few negative ones on our lives. Some may think, "What possible relevance could this have on us now?" Winston Churchill once wrote, "The farther back you can look, the farther forward you are likely to see."[6]

As I look back I am so grateful for the lessons learned and that I witnessed the kind of supernatural display of God that, before 1994, I had only read about. I am grateful to Ray Sell for coming here. God really knit our hearts together. As he traveled in Western New York, Canada, and later Massachusetts and Maryland, he always came back or called to share with me, to talk and to pray with me.

Our families also became very close. In October of 1994, we were shocked to learn that Ray had been diagnosed with leukemia. The disease was far advanced, and doctors did not give him much hope, even with treatment. He did not want to put his young wife and family through the long drawn-out agony of chemotherapy. He insisted that either he would be healed, or he would go home to be with the Lord.

We all prayed fervently for healing. We had gained such hope after the healing of the girl with leukemia. However, it came to a point when Ray knew that he would go home instead. I visited with him in a hospital in Florida, just days before he died.

Revival Belongs to God

It was a difficult time for me. He was a good friend and a brother. His ministry had meant so much to our church. Even though he was younger than I, he was like a mentor in revival for me. He also considered me as a father in the faith. He had mentored me in how to receive the anointing, and I had mentored him in his dealings with other pastors and churches. I had hoped he would continue to be there in our ongoing revival. I felt a deep loss when he died, but I also knew that Ray didn't own this revival. I didn't own it. It was a move of God and I chose to look towards Him for the future of our church.

My ultimate purpose is to glorify God. The more I worship God, the more I fall in love with Him. I know Him now more personally and intimately than ever before. I'm desperate not to miss out on what He is doing now or what He is about to do.

In regards to revival, I fully agree with the words of Charles Colson: "Only God can bring revival, and when it comes we may be surprised. It may not make life easier, but harder. Still if we have any expectation or hope that He will so favor us, we best get down to serious and sacred business. And the place to begin, as Jesus commanded, is with repentant hearts."[7]

The Do's and Don'ts of Revival

In any move of God we need to allow the Holy Spirit to empower and refresh us, but we also need to allow Him to help us fulfill God's vision for our church. Balance has always been very important to me. My staff and I developed a list of renewal "do's and don'ts" that kept us in balance:

1. Don't criticize those who don't move in renewal. You may win them over if you are gentle and patient with them. Many have come around after initial skepticism.

2. Don't be defensive about a move of God; you don't own it. I encouraged my leaders to explain as much as they were able to explain, but I told them to resist feeling threatened if someone was critical. If this move lasts, it would prove itself.

3. Allow God to bless other churches through the renewal in your church. Do not covet another pastor's sheep. Allow them to come, encourage them to go back to their own church and tell them to tithe to their home church. Bless them and speak well of their church and pastor. Bless any pastor or leader who attends your revival meetings. Impart to them freely what the Lord has given you.

4. Don't forsake the goals of the church, but let renewal strengthen and enhance them. Renewal is not the destination, but it is the wind that propels the church to its destination.

5. Hold a special renewal service during the week. Keep Sunday morning services "business as usual" as much as possible, but allow the Holy Spirit to introduce change slowly and naturally.

6. Encourage people to come to the special services, but don't pressure them to receive prayer. Just being in the presence of the Lord and sitting and soaking in His love, helps people learn to receive from Him.

7. Don't make people feel inferior if they are skeptical. Let them taste and see for themselves that the Lord is good and that He wants to bless them with His manifest presence.

8. Strongly encourage your lay leadership to attend Holy Spirit services. To be a leader requires commitment to be on the same page as the pastor. If the church is to be led by the Spirit, leaders need to be together in one place and in one accord. The church started that way; it needs to continue that way.

9. Be very selective about who will pray for people. The Bible instructs to be careful about the laying on of hands. The church leadership needs to be selective in who ministers to the sheep.

10. Let pastoral staff be seen to receive prayer publicly. Pastors lead more by their example than by their words. They need to model and show how to receive from the Lord.

11. Give Bible-based teachings on renewal and revival. Revival and renewal are not a new phenomena. The Old and New Testament are filled with instances of supernatural moves of God.

12. Teach Church revival history. There is nothing new under the sun. The Lord may use different methods, but He never changes. What He has done in the past helps us to be prepared and understand what He does in the present.

13. Don't throw out your church programs. Look at renewal as a forum to enhance your ministries such as the youth group, Sunday school, the worship team, ushering, etc.

14. Teach doctrine and foundational truths. The deeper our roots, the higher we can reach up. Revival does not replace or change doctrine or truth. It helps us to understand them better.

15. Make it your goal to flow and act in unity. With your pastoral and support staff, elders, and lay leadership, the victory comes in unity.

REVIVAL SURVIVAL

To grow through revival remember:

- ❧ Revival flows when leaders are receptive
- ❧ Revival makes some uncomfortable
- ❧ God uses particular people to welcome revival
- ❧ Revival belongs to God not a person or a church

CHAPTER 5

THE POWER OF GOD OR THE GOD OF POWER

W hen revival first came to Love Joy Gospel Church, we did-n't really know much about what God could do with a group of people who were yielded to Him. We were in need of much teaching, but Ray Sell, who had brought us the revival, was no longer with us.

We were grateful for Rev. Bill Wilson, Ray Sell's pastor from Spring Hill, Florida, who soon began to travel as an evangelist, picking up where Ray had left off. Bill's ministry was exciting, powerful, and filled with good teaching and preaching from the Word and the demonstration of God's power. He taught us to "believe the Bible on purpose."

At one of his meetings I noticed a tall, dignified couple in the audience whom I had never seen before. I noticed them again during the ministry time. When Bill Wilson prayed for people, things could get wild and we had people strewn all around the sanctuary. The couple was standing, awestruck, near the sound booth, just watching. After the ministry time, I introduced myself and found out their names. They were Larry and Rita Diebold. I was curious what had brought them to our church.

Larry and Rita had heard about Love Joy through an article from the *Spread the Fire* Magazine from Toronto Airport Christian Fellowship. The interesting thing was that they had received this article in the mail from a friend who lived in Japan. Larry and Rita were Lutheran and had never seen anything like what they witnessed that night. They were intrigued enough to come back the next day, and the next. They're still at Love Joy today. In fact, Rita is on staff as our receptionist.

John Shiver is another pastor who had known Ray Sell and had been touched by God through the ministry of Rodney Howard-Browne. John Shiver, Bill Wilson, and Ray Sell had prayed for revival weekly for three years in the early nineties. God had given John the commission to "go and help prepare the Church for what God was desiring to send: a great outpouring of the Holy Spirit which would result in the greatest revival the earth has ever witnessed."

John began to itinerate and preach revival. John's preaching style could not have been more different from Bill's, but the demonstration of power was the same. He preached with narrative theology, using parables and stories to vividly bring the point across. John is a humble man who takes no glory away from God, but God's glory and presence come in an awesome way when he preaches and ministers.

Signs and wonders follow his preaching of the Word and many people get saved. Whenever he comes to our church, he seems to have his hand on the pulse of the church and delivers just what God wants to impart at that particular time. He encourages the leadership and leaves the church with lasting fruit and in a better place.

We even had a week of revival meetings with Bazil Howard-Browne, Rodney's brother, fresh from South Africa. He was a bold man who had been changed by the anointing into a powerful preacher and carrier of God's presence.

Our South African connection continued with Dr. Leon van Rooyen. He brought an apostolic teaching ministry that impacted our people and taught them to receive the fullness of what God had for them. He refreshed us and renewed in us the desire to receive God's joy.

Each time we had revival meetings it was a stretching time for us. Often issues would arise with one person or another as God brought up areas that such individuals needed to deal with. Sometimes the first few days of revival would be very uncomfortable. A staff member, a leader, or even myself would at first not be able to receive as much out of the meetings as we had hoped. It could be a hard thing to see everyone else around you drunk in the spirit, filled with joy, rolling on the floor with laughter, while God was working a spiritual circumcision inside of you. Soon we realized that it was the flesh that rose up, and those times were needed for us to die to ourselves, and be transformed from glory to glory.

Much of what we learned, we gleaned from Rodney Howard-Browne. Judy and I attended some of his meetings around the country and we read his books. What follows in this chapter are teachings I learned and adopted from him.

Revival is About Presence

Early on in revival I began to understand that the real issue was not whether or not we want the power of God, but whether we really want the presence of God in our lives. God is seeking to build character in us, the character of His Son!

We have the presence of God, not *instead* of His power, but because of His power. The anointing of the Holy Spirit is not just a one-time touch; it is a transformed life-a life that is yielded daily to the Holy Spirit's control. As the apostle Paul wrote to the Galatians, "I have been crucified with Christ; it is no longer I who live, but Christ lives in me; and the life which I now live in the flesh I live by faith in the Son of God, who loved me and gave Himself for me" (Galatians 2:20).

With similar words, Mark 8:34 quotes Jesus as saying: "Whoever desires to come after Me, let him deny himself, and take up his cross, and follow Me."

This is our calling, that we not just live for ourselves, but that the Lord might live His life through us and that we would become carriers of His presence.

Moses knew that the only thing that would make us different and unique from anyone else in the world would be the manifest presence of God revealed in our midst.

His Abiding Presence More Than Just a Touch

Knowing Jesus is important, but having His presence is essential. The presence of the Lord is not an occasional touch from Him, with which so many Christians become satisfied- it is to know His closeness and His power in our daily lives.

The presence of God is a continual filling of the Holy Spirit so that we abide in Him each day. This is the only way that true Christianity can be distinguished from all other religions on earth. Christianity is not just knowing or trying to live by certain doctrines, it is becoming the temple of the Holy Spirit.

Early in my walk with the Lord, I learned the principle of spending time with Him from Paul Johansson, my spiritual mentor, advisor, and friend. Paul helped me to understand Mark 3:13. When Jesus gave His disciples the authority to preach, heal and cast out demons, the first thing He did was call them to Himself. Scripture says, "And He went up on the mountain and called to Him those He Himself wanted. And they came to Him. Then He appointed twelve, that they might be with Him and that He might send them out to preach, and to have power to heal sicknesses and to cast out demons" (Mark 3:13-16).

Revival Power Flows Out of a Relationship with Jesus

They did not operate in power aside from their relationship with Jesus. They operated in power because they had been called to Him first, "And He called the twelve to Himself, and began to send them out two by two, and gave them power over unclean spirits" (Mark 6:7).

This concept is revealed again in the example of Peter and John standing before the council: "When they saw the courage of Peter and John and realized that they were unschooled, ordinary men, they were astonished and they took note that these men had been with Jesus" (Acts 4:13).

Peter or John's intellectual ability was not what caught the attention of these men - it was that *they had been with Jesus.* Those who have been in fellowship with the Lord have a noticeable quality. The fruit of the Spirit is love, joy, peace, patience, kindness, goodness, faithfulness, gentleness, and self-control. Such fruit reflects the presence of God and demonstrates the power of God. Ephesians 5:17-18 says, "Therefore do not be unwise, but understand what the will of the Lord is. And do not be drunk with wine, in which is dissipation; but be filled with the Spirit."

The Greek word for "filled" is "pleroo," which literally means to be "continually filled." This is not a one-time experience. You must be filled with the Holy Spirit daily. Each day we need to submit to the Spirit's control and guidance. Each day we need the anointing of the Holy Spirit.

Revival Brings the Anointing

What is the anointing? The anointing is not some mystical something out there. Rather it is the personality, presence, and power of God manifested in our lives. We could say that the anointing is the manifest presence of God.

The *omnipresence* and the *manifest presence* of God are two different things. The Lord is omnipresent but He is not manifesting or displaying His power everywhere. When God's power does manifest, something happens. We read in Luke 5:17, that the power of the Lord was present to heal. When God walks in, something happens, and something takes place.

The anointing is tangible and we can feel it. I try to allow the Holy Spirit to come and have His way in my ministry, during church services, when I'm out visiting the sick, or when I'm counseling. When I give up control, He comes and manifests Himself and touches the lives of individuals in a wonderful way. It's not our power, it is His; it's not our ability, it is His. He wants us to rely upon Him and trust Him to work through us. Jesus said, "Freely ye have received, freely give" (Matt. 10:8). He said, "Behold, I give unto you power to tread on serpents and scorpions, and over all the power of the enemy" (Luke 10:19).

Anointed to minister. Rodney Howard-Browne says, "The anointing is the supernatural equipment to get the job done. God will never call someone to do something without equipping them with the necessary tools to get the task done. Just like a mountain climber has to have the right boots and equipment, so we, if we would be able ministers of the new covenant, need the anointing."[8]

The Holy Spirit is the power agent of God -active in the world today and available to us who are saved. Power and the Holy Spirit are inseparable. We cannot have "spiritual power" without the Holy Spirit, and we cannot have the Holy Spirit without having His power, which is His ability, efficiency, and might. Acts 1:8 says, "But you shall receive power when the Holy Spirit has come upon you..."

Anointed to do God's work. Regarding this verse, Rodney Howard-Browne says, "This is a personal promise, but you shall receive power. Christ gave us a promise of the impartation of His mighty power, the promise of the anointing of the Holy Spirit. The anointing is God's ability upon man to perform the works of God. The anointing is not based on a man's education, or the lack of it.

"On the contrary, I have seen some very unqualified people minister under the greatest anointing. Sometimes natural ability and talent hinder the individual from being used of God because they are relying on their ability, not on His. God takes the foolish things of the world to confound the wise."[9]

Why is it that some people never sense the presence of God? Howard-Browne says, "I asked the Lord one day why some never sensed His presence. He said it was because many are so caught up in the affairs of this life that their thought life is far from Him. Most of their waking moments are taken up with the things of the natural. They never spend any time in worship or in communication with the Lord. It's almost like they are on another wavelength."[10]

It's like having a radio and wanting to listen to a certain station, and then not tuning in to the correct frequency. You'll never pick up the message. If you make the adjustment, suddenly the signal will come through loud and clear.

Anointed for power in our daily lives. Why do we need the power of God's Spirit in our daily lives? When the Lord prayed for His disciples on the night before His crucifixion, He explained, "As Thou (Father) hast sent Me into the world, even so have I also sent them into the world" (John 17:18).

Also, Acts 10:38 says "...God anointed Jesus of Nazareth with the Holy Ghost and with power who went about doing good, and healing all that were oppressed of the devil, for God was with him." He has sent us just as He was sent: to do good and heal all who are oppressed of the devil, for God is with us.

REVIVAL POWER

The power of God through revival comes:

- In His Presence
- Out of a Personal, Daily Relationship with Jesus
- Through His Anointing
- To Minister
- To Do God's Work in the World
- To Live in the Real World with the
- Character of Christ

REVIVAL POEMS

CHAPTER 6

LEARNING TO FORGIVE

O ne of the saddest things that happened during the revival was that a number of pastors in the area began to criticize our church and me in particular.

God's glory and His wonderful presence was in the church, but some could not accept this as a genuine move of God. I began to hear of churches that were forbidding their people to come and visit Love Joy.

What were we to do? Even though we were crushed by their criticism and judgment, I knew we needed to forgive and release them if God were ever to use us to have an influence on them down the road. I was hopeful that they would eventually be able to receive what we had. Mark Twain said, "Forgiveness is the fragrance the violet sheds on the heel that has crushed it."[11]

Forgive Those Who Speak Against You

Gerald Fry says, "Any study of revival will reveal that two elements are always evident in every revival - unity and prayer."[12]

I began to forgive anyone that was speaking against us. I quoted Isaiah 54:17, "No weapon formed against you shall prosper, and every tongue which rises against you in judgment you shall condemn. This is the heritage of the servants of the LORD, and their righteousness is from Me, says the LORD."

Refuse to Condemn Others

I did not condemn people, but in prayer I condemned their words of judgment. I taught my people not to be haughty and not to look down on anyone who was not yet receiving what we were getting. Over and over, I spoke to them to love, to encourage, to inspire, but never to react in judgment.

At renewal meetings we always told the visitors that their tithe belonged to their local church, not to Love Joy. We would accept their offerings but we insisted that they pay the tithe at their own storehouse. Some accused us of stealing their sheep, but we were not interested in having a lot of transfer growth from other churches. We wanted unchurched people to come.

Encourage Leaders from Other Churches

During a week of revival meetings with Evangelist John Shiver, I noticed a young man in attendance who seemed intensely interested. After the meeting, he pulled me aside because he wanted to talk to me. He introduced himself as Pastor Jon Hasselback. I didn't know him, but I knew of him. He pastored a nearby church and had been one of our critics. With tears in his eyes, he pleaded with me to forgive him for his criticism of me and our church. He was so hungry for God and wanted so much to receive what he saw in our meeting. He came back each day and was powerfully touched.

At a later date, he apologized to me publicly in front of two hundred leaders for the way he had spoken about me. The amazing thing is that all but one of the pastors that spoke against the revival and against me came either personally or publicly and asked for forgiveness. And some, like Jon Hasselback, even came to me with tears.

Soon after, they each began to experience revival in their own services as well. Now, we are all working together in this move of God, for His glory. So instead of condemning other churches and those who condemned us, we encouraged others to seek after God and revival for their own lives and churches.

When you find yourself in revival, be careful not to look down on those who have not experienced what you have. Delight yourself in God's move in your own life, and be loving and sensitive to others, even when they criticize and decry what you are doing.

FORGIVING LOVE

Revival requires that we:

- Forgive those who judge and criticize us
- Work for unity and love in the Body of Christ
- Accept apologies when others offer them
- Encourage other church leaders instead of condemn them
- Refuse to be haughty about what God is doing in our midst

CHAPTER 7

RECEIVING WISE COUNSEL

S cripture clearly declares that we need to walk in authority in the power of the Holy Spirit. Zechariah 4:6 says, "So He answered and said to me, 'This is the word of the LORD to Zerubbabel: 'Not by might, nor by power, but by My Spirit,' says the LORD of hosts.'"

When revival first came, those of us who were touched by it gained a fresh understanding of the authority and the power that were now available to us. God began to demonstrate this power in a new and awesome way through me and through others on our team. I can identify with 1 Corinthians 2:1-5, "And I, brethren, when I came to you, did not come with excellence of speech or of wisdom declaring to you the testimony of God. For I determined not to know anything among you except Jesus Christ and Him crucified. I was with you in weakness, in fear, and in much trembling. And my speech and my preaching were not with persuasive words of human wisdom, but in demonstration of the Spirit and of power, that your faith should not be in the wisdom of men but in the power of God."

Revival Manifests the Power of the Holy Spirit. It became obvious that the Holy Spirit was demonstrating His power through me during church services, in counseling sessions, during deliverances, or in whatever else I was doing. What was not so obvious was a principle I had learned long ago and applied during this time. It was the principle of receiving wise counsel. I may move in the authority and power of the Holy Spirit, but I still need to submit to the counsel and correction of the elders of our church, and those who are over me in the Lord.

I am very grateful to Elim Bible Institute and Elim Fellowship. Their leadership has always demonstrated this principle in a remarkable way; as Proverbs 7:17 says, "As iron sharpens iron, so a man sharpens the countenance of his friend."

Revival Leaders Listen to Wise Counsel. I have learned and believe that constructive criticism between friends develops character and helps us to stay on the cutting edge of what God is doing. On the other hand, I have observed some men and women who are "Lone Rangers." They are not willing to receive counsel or criticism. Most, if not all, have gone astray.

When I had the desire to have Ray Sell come to our church, I did not make a decision until I received the approval of my council of elders. This is not because the elders have more authority than I do, but it is because I want our leadership to be in unity. John Maxwell teaches that leadership equals influence. If I desire to move the church in a certain direction, I need to first influence my elders to come alongside. I don't control them in any way, but rather I try my best to persuade them and then trust their godly wisdom.

Revival Submits to Godly Authority. When revival came, in addition to gaining the support of our own elders, I felt that I needed the approval and counsel of the leadership at Elim Fellowship. I was a little nervous about submitting this move to them because it was so good for my church and for me, and I didn't want to risk their rejection of it. I knew though, that I had to do it, and that I could trust the elders at Elim. Through this step of submission, Ray Sell was welcomed at Elim Bible Institute and then at the Elim Fellowship leadership meetings. This opened the door for revival in many parts of the country as pastors were touched by the power of God and took what they received at Elim back to their own churches. To this day we hear pastors and leaders say, "I was at Elim when Ray Sell was there."

Revival Avoids Human Extremes. The Elim Council of Elders unanimously declared the revival a genuine move of God, but they voiced some concerns and cautions. They cautioned us not to elevate a man but to seek the presence of God. They were concerned that some would use manifestations such as falling, laughing, or being drunk in the Spirit, as a sign of superiority, or that they would judge others based on a lack of manifestations. They cautioned us to keep from extremes.

Revival has God's Vision. Paul Johansson compared the purpose God has for a local church to the destination of a sailboat. He cautioned me that revival is not the destination. Revival is the wind in the sails that propels the boat to its destination. He warned me not to lose God's vision of the Church for the sake of revival.

I was grateful for the wise counsel of men who had experienced past moves of the Holy Spirit. It safeguarded us and allowed us to more freely enjoy what God was doing, without fear of going astray.

Revival Leaders Welcome Correction. For many years, I made it a practice to read one chapter of Proverbs each day. There I found the principle of receiving wise counsel. Throughout my walk with the Lord, I have embraced these Scriptures, and when revival came, I again put them into practice.

He who keeps instruction is in the way of life, but he who refuses correction goes astray (Proverbs 10:17).

Where there is no counsel, the people fall; but in the multitude of counselors there is safety (Proverbs 11:14).

The way of a fool is right in his own eyes, but he who heeds counsel is wise (Proverbs 12:15).

By pride comes nothing but strife, but with the well-advised is wisdom (Proverbs 13:10).

Without counsel, plans go awry, but in the multitude of counselors they are established (Proverbs 15:22).

The ear that hears the rebukes of life will abide among the wise. He who disdains instruction despises his own soul, but he who heeds rebuke gets understanding. The fear of the LORD is the instruction of wisdom, and before honor is humility (Proverbs 15:31-33).

REVIVAL RECEIVES WISE COUNSEL

When godly wisdom flows through revival then:

- The Holy Spirit Manifests Power
- Revival Leaders Listen to Wise Counsel
- Revival Submits to Godly Authority
- Revival Avoids Human Extremes
- Revival has God's Vision
- Revival Leaders Welcome Correction

CHAPTER 8

COUNTING THE COST

M any church people have opinions about how the church should be run, but it is the pastor who ultimately has to hear from God. He has the final say. That's great, but pastors need to be sure that their experiences will pass the test of time. Pastors need to lead according to the Word. Pastors alone carry the final responsibility before God.

Count the Cost of Revival. In any Christian endeavor it is important to count the cost before starting out. It is also important to continue counting the cost while going on with God.

When Judy and I heard from God to leave our wonderful and secure position at our first church, we knew we needed to count the cost. We were leaving a 300-member church to take over Love Joy Gospel Church. The larger church had money, people, resources and influence. Love Joy Gospel Church had twenty-five members, no money, very few resources and limited influence. The cost and the risk were great, but we both knew that we had heard from God. God gave us the gift of faith to make the move.

This faith also carried us through the unexpected criticism from friends, relatives, and peers. We heard such things as, "You're crazy to leave a great suburban church to move into the inner city," or "There are so few people, you won't grow" or even simply, "The work will fail." But we knew God was in it, and we went for it. It took a few years to see the fruit, but the cost was well worth it.

When God came in the revival in April of 1994, our people were well prepared, and we didn't immediately have a high cost to pay. As time went on, however, we began to see that there was a cost after all if we were to allow God to continue to move.

Revival has Opponents. After the first few years, even though many people were being saved, backsliders restored, and hundreds of people refreshed, there were a number of opponents. I Corinthians 16:9 says, "For a great and effective door has opened to me, and there are many adversaries." Other translations say, "…and there is much opposition" (NEB); "…and many opponents" (Berkeley); "…and there are many people against me" (Phillips).

The responses of some of our people were interesting. Though most seemed in favor of what God was doing, I noticed a significant number did not come to our weekly renewal services, or to the revival meetings we scheduled every few months. I knew that we needed to continue the meetings in order for God to do a deeper work in our individual lives and in our corporate body.

Leadership Issues will Arise. Because of my continued emphasis on renewal and revival, a few relational and leadership issues arose. Already a handful of families had left the church because of the changes that were happening, but now some close friends in the body and in the leadership began to get "tired" of the revival. It seemed that they were discontent, and whenever they saw me they complained and questioned my judgment or motives. I have learned that there is a big difference between asking a question of the pastor and questioning the pastor.

At one time these friends were able to receive, but now they were in opposition. Their favorite comments were, "When are we going back to the way it was? This revival is getting out of hand" or "You're going too far with this."

Revival Reacts to God Not Man. The decision I had to make was whether I should react to these complaints or stay the course. After much soul searching, prayer, and counsel from my elders and leaders, we decided that at the danger of losing some families, I would continue to allow God to move as He led me. We lost a few more people which caused disappointment because they were close friends, and some of them were influential in the church.

I continued to encourage people to come to the renewal and revival services, and I waited on God for His direction on when to change anything.

In Revival, Some may Leave but God will Bring Increase. Was it worth it? Absolutely! We continued to be touched by the Holy Spirit and we grew numerically. I determined to forgive and release those who had accused me so that they could go on to do what they felt they should do. Bishop Dennis Leonard says, "There will be times when you experience injustice, discrimination and persecution in your life. However, when you are injured by an unjust act, you must be determined in your heart not to let the hurt get down inside your spirit. If you allow the hurt to get on the inside, you are headed towards destruction."[13]

Not everyone will be passionate for revival. Some will find that revival puts them outside of their religious comfort zone. Nonetheless, the barometer of revival constantly reflects what God wants not what religion dictates. Listen carefully to the voice of God, and stay submitted to godly wisdom, authority and counsel. Stay the course of revival to see God's increase.

COUNTING REVIVAL'S COST

The cost of revival:

- If you want Revival, you must count the personal cost and the cost to the Church
- Some will Oppose Revival
- Leadership Issues will Arise in Revival
- Revival must react to God not man
- Some may leave you or the Church in revival, but God will bring an increase

CHAPTER 9

GROWING IN PRAYER

Andrew Murray commented, "It is on prayer that the promises wait for their fulfillment, the kingdom for its coming, the glory of God for its full revelation."[14]

Experiencing revival through a fresh move of the Holy Spirit will produce tremendous joy and release in our personal lives and in our ministries, but it is a big mistake to assume that the presence of revival means we have spiritually arrived. We may be tempted to throw off basic disciplines, like prayer and reading the Bible, because of the great anointing on our lives. We may think, "I'm on a roll, and I don't need that right now."

I even heard a few revivalists say that prayer is not that important during times of revival because God's presence is so tangible. I completely disagree.

Prayer is Essential to Revival. Thank God, I remembered what got me into revival, and I wasn't about to forsake it. Some people say that they have too many "irons in the fire" to pray, but prayer is the fire. When we neglect prayer, the "irons" will soon cool down. Martin Luther said, "I have so much business, I cannot get on without spending three hours daily in prayer."

There are many divine factors in revival, but prayer is the core issue of all of them. It is the great key that starts any move of God. II Chronicles 7:13-14 says, "If My people who are called by My name will humble themselves, and pray and seek My face, and turn from their wicked ways, then I will hear from heaven, and will forgive their sin and heal their land."

Prayer Helps Maintain Revival. I also believe that effective prayer is the key to maintaining a church in vibrant revival. What is effective prayer? It is when we pray out of our relationship with the Lord and not out of duty. Effective prayer happens when we follow the divine pattern Jesus and the writers of the Bible taught us. We need to be students of biblical prayer.

Pray in the Spirit. Scripture commands us to pray in the Spirit (Jude 20). A major part of my prayer life is speaking in tongues or praying in the Spirit. Speaking in tongues is not psychological, but it helps me psychologically. It bypasses the pressures within the mind and emotions and connects me directly to the Spirit, who gives life. It edifies me, builds me up and strengthens me spiritually, mentally, emotionally, and physically. I pray in tongues every day.

Praying in tongues helps me to pray more effectively in English and it helps me to pray for others. Often, I start my prayer time in tongues until I know what direction the Lord takes me in. Then I'll switch to English, and pray with better understanding.

In small corporate prayer meetings, I'll lead the group by praying in tongues until we all begin to flow together in the Spirit.

Personal Prayer Fuels Corporate Revival. My prayer life has many aspects. I pray alone each day; I pray with my wife and with my children; I pray with my staff; I pray corporately with the church and with pastors of other churches. But one of the most rewarding aspects of my prayer life came about in 1988 when Tom Brazell introduced me to Pastor Al Fiebelkorn. Al asked me if he could come and meet with me regularly so that we could pray together. At first I hesitated, as he was Baptist, and did not pray in tongues.

My prayer life flowed with the gifts of the Spirit and especially praying in tongues. I did not want to offend him, but I also did not want to be hindered in the effectiveness and power of my prayer. He persisted though, and I agreed to do it. My weekly meetings with him proved to be one of the most helpful aspects of my Christian walk.

When we started, we bonded in the Spirit; he was baptized in the Holy Spirit and now speaks in tongues and flows in the gifts of the Spirit.

Our time together over the years has broadened beyond prayer. We have a regular meeting each week where we share insights from the Word and talk about our hurts, disappointments, and victories. Al is a man of the Word, and often he'll come to the meeting excited about what the Lord has shown him. We inspire each other and use each other's insights in our sermons. We are accountable to one another.

Meet Together with Others for Prayer. When the revival came to Love Joy, Al was slow to jump in at first, but when he did, it had a great impact on his life and the life of his Church. He got fully revived in his passion for the Lord, in his desire to minister to his congregation, and his ability to worship freely.

After Al and I met alone together each week, my associate, Andy Zack, our youth pastor, Jason Protzman and more recently, Chip Wood, Pastor Kevin Wing, as well as various other pastors, now join us for prayer. This time is so valuable and powerful to each of us that we rarely miss it. We not only pray together, but also exhort and encourage each other and prophesy to one another. We have become vulnerable and depend on each other for accountability, strength, and friendship.

Pray for Leadership in Revival. Another aspect of prayer that strengthens Love Joy Gospel Church and me personally is my Pastor's Prayer Partners Team. We developed this team according to a prayer ministry started by John Maxwell and the Injoy Life Group. I heard about it in early 1995, one year after revival came, and implemented it soon after.

John Maxwell's materials helped us to organize the team, and we've customized his procedures to fit our needs. Dan and Jenny Ohar head up this vital ministry. Dan, who is also an elder, is my personal prayer partner and Jenny is my wife's. We now have over seventy people on the team who pray for Judy and me daily. Wherever I am in the world, or whatever I'm doing, I know that my prayer partners are praying for me. Each month I send them a list of my top prayer needs.

Two or three prayer partners are scheduled to pray with me before each Sunday service. Often their prophetic words confirm my message. They will then pray throughout the worship time during the service. This type of praying we call "praying on the wall." It is a practice we adopted from Eagles' Wings, based on Nehemiah 4:16-18. During this type of prayer, the intercessors are positioned around the perimeter of the congregation. They pray specifically against demonic interference and distractions. They pray for the presence of the Lord to be unhindered among the people. We are constantly in a spiritual war, and my Prayer Partners help to protect my church, my staff, my family, and me.

Pray Before Services. We have several corporate prayer meetings each week, one before each church service and an early morning prayer meeting led faithfully by Andy Zack. Judy, who is our worship pastor, also recently implemented a pre-service "harp and bowl" type of prayer and worship time where prayer and worship freely flow together. This takes place ten minutes before the start of our services. This we also adopted from Eagles' Wings and it helps us to corporately usher in the presence of the Lord before the service even begins.

In the church office, we often pray for each other as the Lord leads. The burdens of ministry can be heavy, so I am careful to anoint, bless, and encourage my staff in prayer, and they do the same for me. They pray for me before I preach, or do any kind of ministry such as critical hospital visits, difficult counseling situations, deliverances, funerals, weddings, etc. Some of my best experiences, revelations, encouragement, and specific answers to prayer have come in this setting.

Wait on God in Prayer. God gave me another insight in waiting on Him. He showed me how to teach our people to make heavenly withdrawals from Him in order to make divine deposits into people's lives. I found this concept beautifully illustrated in the life of Jesus as described in Luke 5:15-18, "However, the report went around concerning Him all the more; and great multitudes came together to hear, and to be healed by Him of their infirmities. So He Himself often withdrew into the wilderness and prayed. Now it happened on a certain day, as He was teaching that there were Pharisees and teachers of the law sitting by, who had come out of every town of Galilee, Judea, and Jerusalem. And the power of the Lord was present to heal them."

At this time Jesus was already very popular in His ministry. People flocked to Him for healing and to hear Him speak. It would have been easy for Him to neglect His time of prayer and His time of withdrawing into the wilderness. He knew He needed to withdraw from people in order to make a withdrawal from the Father for what He needed most for the people. When He did, the presence of the Lord was present to heal them. If we want people to hear us, we need to hear from Him first.

Spiritual Breakthrough in Revival Requires Prayer. Intercession and prayer are the keys to breakthrough into stronger realms of anointing. Prayer releases God's power for me. The power released through prayer, accompanied by God's presence, is the force that gives me the strength to proceed with what God is calling me to do.

GROWING IN PRAYER

As you pray during revival, remember:

- Prayer is essential not peripheral to revival
- Prayer helps maintain revival
- Pray in the Spirit
- Meet together with others for prayer
- Pray for leadership in revival
- Pray before services
- Wait on God in prayer
- Pray for spiritual breakthrough

CHAPTER 10

WORKING IN THE HARVEST

"It's time for the harvest and it's time to begin mobilizing the end-time harvesters." That was the word of the Lord to me during the summer of 1999. I felt that the Lord was beginning to do something new.

In July, we were having a series of meetings with evangelist John Shiver. I had scheduled John to be with us for one week. He began the first meeting by relating what had recently happened when he preached at Surfside Beach, South Carolina and then at Dave Mullin's Church in Manchester, Connecticut. Apparently God had started to manifest His glory with physical signs that John had never seen before. It started with little sprinkles of gold dust that appeared here and there, on the pulpit, on the carpet, and on people's hands. John tried to ignore it, but it increased.

Manifestations of Glory. I had heard of the gold before. In May, Beverly Wilson of Spring Hill, Florida held a women's conference here at our church and mentioned that gold dust had started appearing at their meetings in Florida. My wife then began to see gold dust on her shoes and hands and on the hands of others on the worship team. Other women told me they had sprinkles of gold on their hands occasionally. I couldn't see it.

John Shiver, after preaching, started ministering to our people in the meetings. He did not pray for them the same way he had been doing for the last five years. He did not seem so interested in having them just filled with the Holy Spirit, but instead held their hands in his and asked God to saturate them and show them His glory. He kept looking at their hands. I didn't know what to do, so I just stood in the prayer line and waited for him to pray for me. When he did, I kept my eyes shut and just yielded to the Holy Spirit.

Several times, while I was resting in the Spirit, John came back to me and prayed again for me, and then he would move on. I could hear him ask people, "Have you ever had gold in your hands?" I didn't hear their answer.

I really didn't know what to make of it. During the meeting on the second night, John asked those people who had seen gold or oil on their own body to please stand up. Many did, including my wife. John preached about the gospel that must not only be heard and felt, but must be seen as well. He gave Scripture after Scripture from the New Testament, where the gospel was preached with signs and wonders following. The gospel was seen in the book of Acts, not just heard.

Five years ago, I began to experience the Gospel at a new level; it was as though I was learning how to "feel" it. I learned to receive the new wine-a fresh sense of the deep joy and presence of the living God. That particular period of time had been a stretching time for me, and I never thought that I would have to stretch that much again. Yet here it was again, God was manifesting Himself visibly with gold and oil.

I didn't know if I wanted that. I had taken a lot of criticism in 1994, when many friends in the ministry thought I had gone crazy for allowing such chaos as laughing and rolling on the floor to happen in our church. I could already hear the voices again speaking of emotionalism and sensationalism. They were saying "Show it to me in the Scriptures." Would I have to defend something that I didn't even want or understand? The very morning that I woke up with those questions, John Shiver shared with me his own feelings. He said that he had never asked for this, but that this is what the Father was doing. And since he didn't start it, he didn't have to defend it. That morning, God challenged me to get out of His way.

I remembered a sermon I had preached about how leaders of a previous move of God often have a hard time receiving the next move of God. I had preached it as a warning to others, now I had to heed the warning myself. I repented and asked God to do whatever He wanted. As soon as I yielded myself completely, beads of oil started to appear on my hands. This oil had the fragrance of the anointing oil we used when praying for the sick.

At the next meeting, I followed John during the ministry time and he showed me the gold and oil on people's hands. I saw the wonder on their faces when they realized that God had manifested His glory to them. I saw children awed and skeptics convinced. I was filled with the joy of seeing God at work in others.

Going Out to the Harvest. Our week of meetings ended, but both John and I felt that God wasn't finished with us yet. We extended the meetings for another week. I felt God wanting to do something in our church that would thoroughly turn us inside out. He wanted us to turn outward now. After week two, the number of people coming to the meetings were still increasing, so we extended them again. God now wanted us not so much to come to the meetings for our own renewal, but to bring in the lost and begin taking part in the end-time harvest. John kept repeating, "The renewal is over, revival is next."

God spoke clearly to me that I was to specifically pray for those who were to go out into the harvest. On Thursday night, August 12, we asked only those to come forward who wanted an active part in the end-time harvest. Out of 180 present, at least 150 came forward. The rest came forward for salvation later.

Baptizing New Believers. On Friday, August 13, we prepared to baptize fourteen people who had previously requested to be baptized. John preached a short message and we started to baptize people. He encouraged anyone who had gotten saved the day before to come forward and be baptized. I asked each one to say his or her name and to proclaim, "Jesus is Lord" before going into the waters. John prophesied over many of them, and then our helpers, Pastor Jason Protzman and Rev. Don Swartzlander, baptized them by immersion.

As we came to one young lady, who had come forward in her street clothes, I sensed that she had not yet accepted Jesus as her Savior. I led her in a prayer for salvation before she went into the water. Many more people came up fully clothed. We ran out of towels and had to reuse wet towels several times over. People didn't care. We lost track of how many were baptized because we all became drunk in the Spirit as we were ministering. When we listened to the tape later, we realized that we had baptized thirty people.

We extended the meetings into the fourth week. John continued teaching us about being yielded to God. He taught one night about hurricanes and how they are forever hungry for low barometric pressure. They travel hundreds of miles searching for low pressure. They will skirt around, searching, probing, and seeking for a place to come ashore. However, a system of high pressure will always keep them away.

John likened this to the way the Holy Spirit searches for yieldedness in people and churches. He will search, move, and look for those who don't put up high pressure towards Him, and He will come when we are yielded. John said that five years ago the Holy Spirit was looking for yieldedness, and at that time, it was only the edge of the hurricane that hit us. We yielded then, and now we need to yield again because the hurricane is coming closer.

Those who were offended at laughter put up high pressure and ended up missing what God had wanted to do in them. We yielded to the laughter and conversely experienced the work of God within us. Are we now going to put up high pressure when He comes in a different way? No way! Our prayer was and still is: 'Now, Lord, look on their threats, and grant to Your servants that with all boldness they may speak Your word, by stretching out Your hand to heal, and that signs and wonders may be done through the name of Your holy Servant Jesus.' "And when they had prayed, the place where they were assembled together was shaken; and they were all filled with the Holy Spirit, and they spoke the word of God with boldness" (Acts 4:28-31).

The meetings went on for a total of six weeks. Afterwards, we all wondered how we were able to have handled our families, jobs, and ministries during that time. God had provided all that we needed.

Outward Signs Turn us Outward Toward the Lost. By showing us outward signs, God used this season to turn us outward. He turned us from an inward focus, from the anointing for inward change, to an outward focus, the anointing to minister to our families, our friends, our neighborhoods, and our communities.

Working in the Harvest

In the course of Revival, God turns our Inward Focus, Outward by:

- Manifesting His Glory
- Moving us to go out into the Harvest
- Baptizing New Believers
- Giving us Outward Signs to Move us out Toward the Lost

CHAPTER 11

STAYING THE COURSE

P aul writes in I Corinthians 16:13, "Watch, stand fast in the faith, be brave, be strong." In the midst of revival, we can be tempted to neglect the prayer watch and become caught up in the passion and excitement of what God is doing. We can begin trusting men for leadership instead of being led by God. As persecution and criticism arise, we can be tempted to give up. We can become tired physically, emotionally, and spiritually.

However, if we stay the watch of prayer, continue to trust God, confront criticism with humility and speaking truth in love, and find our rest and strength in the Lord, we will stay the course and live in the Spirit of revival.

As of this writing, it has been almost eight years since Ray Sell came to our church and God sovereignly moved us into revival. In Luke 19, Jesus said, "...you did not know the time of your visitation." I am so happy that our leaders, elders, and congregation recognized the time of our visitation and embraced the move of God.

Are things still as exciting as they were eight years ago? Not all the time. They are still powerful, and the presence of God is real, but it doesn't come as a surprise to us anymore. We don't take God's presence for granted, but we can be assured that if we ask and if we yield, He will come.

When the baptism of the Spirit and speaking in tongues was restored to the Church at Azuza Street in the early nineteen hundreds, it came as such a surprise that the Christian world was ablaze. Is speaking in tongues still as exciting as it was then? Yes and no. We do it now more than ever, so it's not surprising anymore. Just so, the joy and presence and anointing of God that was restored to us in 1994, is still with us. We have learned how to tap into it and receive it so that we can pour it out to others.

The Fruit of Revival. I now see a changed church. Before 1994, we needed to learn how to be open to receive the anointing. Now many are flowing in the anointing and are using it to minister to others. We have seen more high school graduates go to Bible school in the last few years than ever before. We have had a marked increase in short-term mission involvement by the teens of our church.

I am also raising up young leaders in the church through a discipleship process. As these young people learn to minister under the power and anointing of the Holy Spirit, revival will last. We have recognized that in times of transition, we sometimes find it harder to find the river of God, which is the flow or the move of the Holy Spirit. Transitions are like the turning of the river. We may need to move in a different direction in order to stay with what God is doing.

These transitional seasons also can seem to us like a lull in the wind. Suddenly, I may become aware that what had propelled us forward at breakneck speed has quieted down. Like the captain of a sailboat, I may wonder if we'll ever move that fast again. At those times, I can't pretend that things are the same, and I can't keep the outward manifestations going, to make it seem like God is moving. At those times, I need to just encourage our people to do what we know is right. Pray, worship, seek His face, stay in the Word, care for the flock, and look for the wind to blow again.

The Flow of the Spirit's Anointing Continues. I found that even when the intensity of the move of God is not there, the anointing He has placed in me does not go away. Those who were thirsty for God and had learned to receive His anointing, His power, and His presence still can receive them during the lull.

In 1994, God took us from ministering out of duty into a time of just receiving His joy, His blessing, and His passion. Then, starting in 1999, He moved us from receiving to giving-out. That transition was difficult at first, but He is faithful. As pastors, we are now confident that we are equipping the saints for the work of the ministry with an anointing that makes a difference. We are activating their spiritual gifts and releasing them to the world. Now we know how to receive and how to give out. Both aspects are needed all the time.

Moving in the Miraculous. In May of 2002, at our annual Elim Fellowship Leadership Meeting, Frank Damazio spoke about moving in the miraculous. His message was a confirmation of what God had been speaking to me. God had already confirmed His still small voice through bold prophetic words by credible prophets, but when I heard Frank Damazio, I knew that now was the time to trust God more than ever before, to confirm His word through signs, wonders and miracles.

I began to prepare the Church to be ready to see miracles in us, miracles around us, and miracles through us. God is faithful. Many reports are coming in that God is doing what He said He would do, and our people are becoming bold to allow Him to use them beyond the walls of the Church. We have reports coming in of miracles at home, in home groups, in hospitals, at the work place, and of course, right here at church.

Our young people are more passionate than ever. We started a Generation Service for twelve to twenty-four year olds, and there we see the word of the prophet Joel being fulfilled that your sons and your daughters will prophesy. Our youth leaders are guiding this generation into their own experience with God's presence and glory.

Staying Hungry and Thirsty for God. Though we have had times of dryness, our hunger and thirst for the things of God have always brought us back to the river of God. I am determined to stay hungry for God and to look to Him for direction. I do not ever want to become spiritually stagnant, choosing to remain in what God did in the past. Because of God's faithfulness to bring me into revival, I can trust him with implementing new things in my ministry. I am able to discern what is from Him and run with it.

I am so glad to be connected with Elim Fellowship, which, since its founding by Ivan Spencer, has desired to be like a willow in the wind, experiencing and yielding to the wind of the Spirit whenever God blows it across the earth. The move of God is a continual flow. If we stay in the Spirit's river, we can have continuous revival.

STAYING THE COURSE

In order the stay the course and continue to live in the Spirit of revival, we must:

- Stay the Watch of Prayer
- Trust God to Lead us Forward
- Be Courageous as God Continues to do New Things
- Be Strong and not Grow Weary Physically, Emotionally or Spiritually
- Continue to Bear Spiritual Fruit
- Be Open to the Continual Flow of the Spirit's Anointing
- Move in the Miraculous
- Stay Hungry and Thirsty for God

Chapter 12

Looking Ahead to the Future

My continuing vision is that Love Joy Gospel Church will be a culturally and ethnically diverse church that reaches out to our own area and to the world.

The process for achieving multiethnic unity and racial reconciliation within the Church is often slow because the Church's unity is based, not on superficial tolerance, not on economic issues, not on fear or guilt, but on authentic love and relationships. As such, loving relationships cannot be mandated or forced on people, but they must be modeled, nurtured, and allowed to grow naturally. As a Pastor, I can help to facilitate this process by intentionally focusing on unity.

Seek Intentional Unity. Jesus prayed for intentional unity. "I do not pray for these alone, but also for those who will believe in Me through their word; that they all may be one, as You, Father, are in Me, and I in You; that they also may be one in Us, that the world may believe that You sent Me" (John 17:20-21).

In his book, *Prepare the Way*, Robert Stearns gives twelve spiritual signposts for the new millennium, one of which is "One Body, Diverse Members." He writes: "The next generation will be intentional in reconciliation. It will embrace the strengths found in other cultures and seek to honor others and learn from them."[15]

Our natural tendency is to examine differences and weaknesses in each other, rather than embracing strengths. We are all born of the same flesh, and as Christians, if indeed we are born again, we are all born of the same Spirit. Jesus calls us His brethren. "For both He who sanctifies and those who are being sanctified are all of one, for which reason He is not ashamed to call them brethren" (Hebrews 2:11).

If He, who is so far above us, is willing to identify with us, we must identify with those who are different than us but are born of the same Spirit. Isaiah 54:2 says, "Enlarge the place of your tent and let them stretch out the curtains of your dwellings. Do not spare, lengthen your cords and strengthen your stakes. For you shall expand to the right and to the left and your descendants will inherit the nations and make the desolate cities inhabited." The New Living Translation says, "Enlarge your house, build an addition, spread out your home."

Just having the river flow in our own lives though is not enough. We need to see people saved and different ethnic groups come together in the Church, because it's in that kind of unity where God commands a blessing.

Isaiah 56:7-8 says, "For My House shall be called a House of Prayer for all nations. The Lord God who gathers the outcast of Israel says 'Yet I will gather to Him others besides those who are gathered to Him.'" He will gather others that we know nothing about. Maybe we don't know their culture or the customs of their race, but God is going to invite them in.

Reject prejudice. In order for the Church to be united across racial boundaries, we need to enlarge our hearts to receive those that are different from us. The problem is that many of us deal with prejudice in our lives. Webster says that prejudice is "a judgment or opinion formed before the facts are known, preconceived ideas, favorable or more usually, unfavorable." It's usually suspicion, intolerance, or irrational hatred of other races, regions, people groups, or occupations.

Bishop Dennis Leonard writes, "Prejudice is a strategy from Satan to destroy God's command to love one another." Prejudice is a belief that race is a reason for certain undesirable human traits. Prejudice is a feeling that one race is superior to another race. All degrees of it are based on misguided power and fear. And prejudice affects everyone in some fashion, whether it's admitted or not. He also writes, "Racism, prejudice, and hatred are works of the flesh."

When we are born-again, the Lord expects us to overcome our flesh and become loving, forgiving, and accepting. We are to love our brothers and sisters no matter who they are. We are to pray for and win all kinds of people to the Lord. We are coming to the end of the age and Jesus said in John 17:20-23, "I do not pray for these alone, but also for those who will believe in Me through their word; *that they all may be one*, as You, Father, are in Me, and I in You; that they also may be one in Us, that the world may believe that You sent Me. And the glory which You gave Me I have given them, that they may be one just as We are one: I in them, and You in Me; that they may be made perfect in one, and that the world may know that You have sent Me, and have loved them as You have loved Me."

People of different nationalities, races, creeds and geographic places are looking for someone to come and bandage their wounds, as the Good Samaritan did to the man who was robbed and left for dead. He poured on oil and wine, a healing element to soothe those wounds. Then he put him on his donkey and took him to an inn and took care of him.

Jesus was speaking into a racial situation with this story. He was speaking of the need for reconciliation and love between ethnic groups. He knew the Scripture verse that said "My house shall be called a House of Prayer for all ethnoi" (i.e. nations, races, and different cultures).

Jesus said, "Go and do likewise." Jesus commended the hated foreigner, the Samaritan, who was capable of compassion. Not only did he have compassion, but he brought action with it. Jesus said "Blessed are the peacemakers." It's more than just saying, "I'm a peacemaker," or "I have compassion." We need to put action into our words.

Even before September 11, Robert Stearns wrote: "We have only to look at the global tensions to see how desperate we are for peace. Israel and the Palestinians, Northern Ireland, racial tensions in South Africa. Hindus versus Muslims in India. Racial strife throughout America. It seems that the more we talk about multicultural acceptance the less tolerance we have toward one another. In the midst of this cultural war zone, Jesus has called believers to be the peacemakers. He has called us to become a force for justice and peace in the midst of troubled times."[16]

Racial issues have become a whole lot more complicated since September 11. On a personal level, we need to show the same love as the Samaritan did, to the Jew. In *KAIROS* Magazine, Wesley Campbell writes: "On the personal level, no Christian is to respond with hatred, prejudice, or personal retaliation. Jesus' words to 'love your enemies and pray for those who persecute you,' are still as binding as when they were first given to the disciples... As individuals we must have no place for hatred of Muslims or for bullying those who believe differently than we do. We are called to pray for Muslims and people of every religion. We are further called to reach out to the poor, irrespective of their faith or creed."[17]

Fight Evil. This is the role of every Christian. On another level though, we need to fight. Wes Campbell continues: "On the other hand, the governments and authorities that are instituted by God also become for God the avengers who bring judgment on those who do evil. 'For rulers and governing authorities are ministers of God to you for good. But if you do what is evil, be afraid; for it does not bear the sword for nothing; for it is a minister of God, an avenger who brings wrath upon the one who practices evil'" (Romans 13:3-4).[18]

On a spiritual level, we as the Church need to fight as well. God sees His people as weapons of war. "You are My battle-ax and weapons of war: for with you I will break the nation in pieces. With you I will destroy kingdoms" (Jeremiah 51:20).

The war we fight in the Church though is not a physical war and our weapons are not physical weapons. "For though we walk in the flesh, we do not war according to the flesh. For the weapons of our warfare are not carnal but mighty in God for pulling down strongholds, casting down arguments and every high thing that exalts itself against the knowledge of God, bringing every thought into captivity to the obedience of Christ, and being ready to punish all disobedience when your obedience is fulfilled" (II Corinthians 10:3-6).

Even though pastoring a multi-ethnic church does have its challenges, I am believing God to help me and our church to do what needs to be done so that people of all races will feel welcome here. Heaven is a place where all races and cultures worship God and live together in unity. So my prayer is, "Thy kingdom come, Thy will be done on earth as it is in heaven."

We also want to continue extending the influence of the Kingdom of God in the Western New York region. After revival first started in 1994, we planted a church on the West Side of Buffalo. I would like to plant at least one more church in our area. Even though there are many good churches in Western New York, there are only a few that significantly move in the gifts of the Spirit and allow the supernatural to occur on a regular basis. For God to transform our city, and our region, we will need many more churches like that.

The Lord made it clear to me that to move into what He wants to do in this region, I need to move in the supernatural. In September 2000, Bill Hamon the prophet spoke these words over me, "The Lord says, 'I'm saying you need to release My supernatural, because your calling card is not going to be just a beautiful church, or a nice thing, your calling card is going to be the supernatural. And from this day forward you're moving into your Caanan land. You're moving into the supernatural. You're moving into a release of my power, and I release you into the prophetic, apostolic double portion anointing you have been believing for. And from this day forward, release my power, release my anointing. As you do, I'll release the money, and I'll bring in the people, and I'll activate the purpose, and I'll bring to pass what you've been praying for. If you activate my gifts, and bless my saints, I'll bless you.'"

Expand Missions. Love Joy Gospel Church, from its beginning, has been a missions-giving Church. We can't all go into the mission field, but we can all help to fulfill the Great Commission. God calls individuals to serve as missionaries on the field. They can fulfill that call because God also calls local churches at home to faithfully support them in prayer, and with regular monthly financial contributions. Presently, we support over forty different missionaries. We choose one a week as our missions prayer focus. We pray for them during our Sunday service and then throughout the week. Once a month we publish a missions newsletter for our congregation.

I believe that God has not only called Love Joy to support our missionaries financially, and in prayer, but also to support them with apostolic ministry teams of powerful anointing to both encourage them and help to assist them in bringing spiritual breakthrough to their towns, cities, and nations. Sending apostles, prophets, evangelists, pastors, and teachers in a laser-focused way will cause a quicker and greater release of God's power in these areas.

I see, as another fruit of revival, a greater participation in short-term missions by our congregation. We have sent teams to Egypt and Mexico and team leaders to various parts of the world. We also have sent out full-time missionaries with Wycliffe and Elim.

LOOKING AHEAD TO THE FUTURE

For revival to move steadfastly into the future, we must:

- Seek Intentional Unity
- Reject Prejudice
- Fight Evil
- Expand Missions

Afterword

Giving Thanks

"How lovely is Your tabernacle, O LORD of hosts! My soul longs, yes, even faints For the courts of the LORD; My heart and my flesh cry out for the living God" (Psalm 84:1-2).

I am so grateful for what God has done over these last eight years of revival at our Church. We have experienced numerical and spiritual growth. Many have been saved, and many have recommitted their lives to Christ. Through God's glorious presence we have witnessed signs, and wonders, changed lives, and improved marriages and families. I appreciate all the pastors and missionaries who have allowed me to preach at their churches, or in their mission fields.

At this time in ministry, I find myself hungrier than ever for God to move in a fresh and new way. Again, there are many who need a genuine touch from God in their lives for salvation, deliverance, and healing. I see men, women, youths, singles, and married couples that need a Holy Spirit encounter with God.

When people are strong, the Church will become strong. Luke 5:36-39 speaks very relevantly to where we currently are as a local Church, "Then He spoke a parable to them: 'No one puts a piece from a new garment on an old one; otherwise the new makes a tear, and also the piece that was taken out of the new does not match the old. And no one puts new wine into old wineskins; or else the new wine will burst the wineskins and be spilled, and the wineskins will be ruined. But new wine must be put into new wineskins, and both are preserved. And no one, having drunk old wine, immediately desires new'; for he says, 'The old is better'" (Luke 5:36-39).

In these Scriptures, we see that both the wine and the wineskin are important. Without the wineskin the wine is lost and without the wine, the wineskin is useless. God's desire is for us to be new wineskins that are filled with new wine. I pray that we as leaders along with our church members will be open to what God wants to do in our midst, even if it's not a "wineskin" that we are used to or familiar with.

Throughout the centuries, the Holy Spirit has moved in the Church. In studying past revivals, I have seen that He moves on a particular group of people at different times according to a sovereign act of God and the preparatory work of human hearts. As people and churches prepare themselves to be renewed and revived by the Holy Spirit, He moves upon those people. We are living in days when those events that Jesus prophesied for the end-times seem to be increasing: "wars, rumors of wars, famine, pestilence, and earthquakes" (Matthew 24:6).

Terrorism has come to our country, and is in all probability here for a long time. We need God; we need revival; we need an end-time harvest of souls. General Douglas MacArthur once said, "History fails to record a single precedent in which nations subject to moral decay have not passed into political and economic decline. There has been either a spiritual awakening to overcome the moral lapse, or a progressive deterioration to ultimate national disaster."[19]

So, this is our continual prayer for living in the Spirit of Revival:

> *Will You not revive us again,*
> *That Your people may rejoice in You?*
> *Show us Your mercy, LORD, And grant us Your salvation.*
> *Surely His salvation is near to those who fear Him,*
> *That glory may dwell in our land*
> (Psalm 85:6-9).

NOTES

[1] Rev. Harold Harding, Prophecy Transcript, (1985)

[2] Dr. Larry Lea, *Could You Not Tarry One Hour?*, (Church on the Rock, 1986) p. 1.

[3] *Could You Not Tarry One Hour?*, p. 12.

[4] Ronald V. Burgio, *Preparing for Revival*, audio tape (Love Joy Gospel Church, 1994)

[5] Edith Adele Veach, *Elim - Living in the Flow* (Elim Bible Institute, 1999) p. 73.

[6] Winston Churchill as quoted by Gerald Fry, *In Pursuit of His Glory*, (Mount Hermon Press, 1999) p. 2.

[7] *In Pursuit of His Glory*, p. 27.

[8] Rodney Howard-Browne, sermon notes, 1985

[9] Browne sermon notes, 1985.

[10] Browne sermon notes, 1985.

[11] Gerald Fry quoting Mark Twain, *In Pursuit of His Glory* (Mount Hermon Press - 1999) p. 61.

[12] In Pursuit of His Glory, p. 62.

[13] Bishop Dennis Leonard, *Building the Dream* (Dennis Leonard Publishing - 2000) p. 20.

[14] Gerald Fry quoting Andrew Murray, *In Pursuit of His Glory* (Mount Hermon Press - 1999) p. 75.

[15] Robert Stearns, *Prepare the Way* (Creation House - 1999) p. 89.

[16] *Prepare the Way*, p. 89.

[17] Wesley Campbell (*KAIROS* Magazine, Jan-Mar 2002) p. 20.

[18] Wesley Campbell in *KAIROS* Magazine, Jan-Mar 2002, p. 20.

[19] Gerald Fry quoting Douglas MacArthur, *In Pursuit of His Glory* (Mount Hermon Press - 1999) p. 147.

BIBLIOGRAPHY

Unless otherwise stated, quotations from the Bible are from the New King James Version Copyright 1982 by Thomas Nelson, Inc.

Bishop Dennis Leonard, *Building the Dream* (Dennis Leonard Publishing, L.L.C. - 2000)

Dr. Larry Lea, *Could You Not Tarry One Hour?* (Church on the Rock - 1986)

Gerald Fry, I*n Pursuit of His Glory* (Mount Hermon Press - 1999)

Wesley Campbell (*KAIROS* Magazine, David Trementozzi, Editor - Jan-Mar 2002)

Robert Stearns, *Prepare the Way* (Creation House - 1999)

Ronald V. Burgio, *Preparing for Revival*, Audio Tape (Love Joy Gospel Church - 1994)

MINISTRY INFORMATION

Pastor Ron Burgio
Love Joy Gospel Church
5423 Genesee St.
Lancaster, NY 14086

Phone: 716-651-0400
Email: rburgio@lovejoy.org
www.lovejoy.org

ADDITIONAL BOOKS
FROM
KAIROS PUBLISHING

The Way of the Thorn - *David Trementozzi*
In brilliant fashion, reminiscent of *Pilgrims Progress*, David Trementozzi squarely faces one of life's central dilemmas - suffering. Drawing on the imagery of Paul's thorn in the flesh, he masterfully weaves a tale that not only brings understanding, but elicits hope.
PUBLISHED IN COOPERATION WITH EVERGREEN PRESS
ISBN 1-58169-097-5 $10.99

One People, Many Tribes - *Dr. Daniel C. Juster*
In this Messianic Jewish perspective on Church history, Dr. Juster describes how the various restoration movements in the history of the Church have served to either hinder or help the Church come into greater levels of New Testament truth.
ISBN 0-9665831-1-6 $9.99

Youth Can Minister - *Bruce & Lynn Latshaw*
Learn how Pastors Bruce and Lynn Latshaw
have successfully nurtured and released ON-
FIRE Christian youth into ministry. If you have
a vision to see qualified youth empowered and
released to impact their generation for Christ,
this book will encourage you and provide work
able ways to implement the vision!
ISBN 0-9674653-0-3 $9.99

Ten Commandments for Success -
Robert I. Winer, M.D.
This book will shake loose false notions about
the most gifted Law Giver in the history of
mankind and reveal vital opportunities for
greater success in every aspect of your life.
ISBN 0-9655180-0-0 $4.99

Making your words Timeless...

Will God's revelation to you this year be lost forever?

Each year, God gives you dynamic and lasting revelation through a series of messages or teachings that need to be preserved as a legacy for the coming generations of new people in your congregation and in other conference and ministry settings where you speak.

Your *kairos* moment of preaching or teaching may never again be preached by you from a pulpit, but it can become a lasting legacy for ongoing inspiration and revelation to others.

Provide your people each year with a book that they can reread over and over again and share with others. Leave a legacy. Develop an outstanding library of ministry resources for your people from what God has spoken to you.

KAIROS PUBLISHING can transform your notes, manuscripts and tapes or CDs into dynamic, cost-effective books for your ministry. KAIROS PUBLISHING can also market your books through the catalogues, magazines and events of Eagles' Wings.

KAIROS PUBLISHING is committed to producing material that will advance the Kingdom of God and call the Body of Christ to a place of intimacy. When God's timing and destiny meet, we believe a Spirit-breathed word comes forth, providing insight through hearts and souls that have been touched by His mighty hand.

KAIROS PUBLISHING is an entity of Eagles' Wings. Eagles' Wings is an international, relational network of believers who are committed to the unity of the Body of Christ, biblical spirituality through a lifestyle of worship and prayer, and the restoration of Israel.

For more information, please contact:

Vanessa Coenraad
Kairos Media
PO Box 450
Clarence, NY 14031
Email: vanessacoenraad@eagleswings.to
Website: www.kairos.us
Tel: 716.759.1058 x23
Fax: 716.759.0731

EAGLES' WINGS

Eagles' Wings is an international relational network of believers, churches and ministries committed to the lifestyle of biblical spirituality through a lifestyle of worship and prayer (Acts 2:42-47), the unity of the Body of Christ (Psalm 133, John 17:21), and the restoration of Israel (Amos 9:11-15).

Eagles' Wings is comprised of a full time staff of thirty, under the leadership of an Advisory Board with Robert Stearns serving as Executive Director. Eagles' Wings has ministered in over thirty nations, and maintains active, ongoing ministry in Honduras and Israel.

PO BOX 450
CLARENCE, NY 14031

TEL: 716.759.1058

FAX: 716.759.0731

VISIT OUR WEBSITE:
www.eagleswings.to